KT-495-651

❧

Ten Sermons
On The
Holy Spirit

❧

Wind and Fire

by
C. H. SPURGEON

AMBASSADOR

Wind and Fire
© Copyright 1995 Ambassador Productions Ltd.

All rights reserved

ISBN   1   898787   31   X

Printed and Published by
AMBASSADOR PRODUCTIONS LTD
Providence House
16 Hillview Avenue,
Belfast, BT5 6JR

CONTENTS

THE COMFORTER

A SERMON

Text.—"But the Comforter, which is the Holy Ghost, whom the Father will send in my name, he shall teach you all things, and bring all things to your remembrance, whatsoever I have said unto you."—John xiv. 26.

GOOD old Simeon called Jesus the consolation of Israel; and so He was. Before His actual appearance, His name was the Day-Star; cheering the darkness, and prophetic of the rising sun. To Him they looked with the same hope which cheers the nightly watcher, when from the lonely castle-top he sees the fairest of the stars, and hails her as the usher of the morn. When He was on earth, He must have been the consolation of all those who were privileged to be his companions. We can imagine how readily the disciples would run to Christ to tell Him of their griefs, and how sweetly with that matchless intonation of His voice, He would speak to them and bid their fears be gone. Like children, they would consider Him as their Father; and to Him every want, every groan, every sorrow, every agony, would at once be carried; and he, like a wise physician, had a balm for every wound; He had mingled a cordial for their every care; and readily did He dispense some mighty remedy to allay all the fever of their troubles. Oh! it must have been sweet to have lived with Christ. Surely sorrows then were but joys in masks, because they gave an opportunity to go to Jesus to have them removed. Oh! would to God, some of us may say, that we could have lain our weary heads upon the bosom of Jesus, and that our birth had been in that happy era, when we might have heard His kind voice, and seen His kind look, when He said ".Let the weary ones come unto me."

But now He was about to die. Great prophecies were to be fulfilled, and great purposes were to be answered, and therefore Jesus must go. It behoved Him to suffer, that He might be made a propitiation for our sins. It behoved Him to slumber in the dust awhile, that He might perfume the chamber of the grave to make it—

> "No more a charnel house to fence
> The relics of lost innocence."

It behoved Him to have a resurrection, that we who shall one day be the dead in Christ, might rise first, and in glorious bodies stand upon earth. And it behoved Him that He should ascend up on high, that He might lead captivity captive; that He might

7

chain the fiends of hell; that He might lash them to His chariot wheels and drag them up high heaven's hill, to make them feel a second overthrow from His right arm when He should dash them from the pinnacles of heaven down to deeper depths beneath. "It is right I should go away from you," said Jesus, "for if I go not away, the Comforter will not come." Jesus must go. Weep, ye disciples. Jesus must be gone. Mourn, ye poor ones who are to be left without a Comforter. But hear how kindly Jesus speaks: "I will not leave you comfortless, I will pray the Father, and He shall send you another Comforter, who shall be with you, and shall dwell in you for ever." He would not leave those few poor sheep alone in the wilderness; He would not desert His children and leave them fatherless. Before He left He gave soothing words of comfort; like the good Samaritan, He poured in oil and wine; and we see what he promised: "I will send you another Comforter—one who shall be just what I have been, yea even more; who shall console you in your sorrows, remove your doubts, comfort you in your afflictions, and stand as My vicar on earth, to do that which I would have done, had I tarried with you."

Before I discourse of the Holy Ghost as the Comforter, I must make one or two remarks on the different translations of the word rendered "Comforter." The Rhemish translation, which you are aware is adopted by Roman Catholics, has left the word untranslated, and gives it "Paraclete." "But the Paraclete which is the Holy Ghost, whom the Father will send in my name, he shall teach you all things." This is the original Greek word, and it has some other meanings besides "Comforter." Sometimes it means the monitor or instructor: "I will send you another monitor, another teacher." Frequently it means "Advocate"; but the most common meaning of the word is that which we have here: "I will send you another *Comforter*." However, we cannot pass over those other two interpretations without saying something upon them.

"I will send you another *teacher*." Jesus Christ had been the official teacher of His saints whilst on earth. They called no man Rabbi except Christ. They sat at no men's feet to learn their doctrines; but they had them direct from the lips of Him who "spake as never man spake." "And now," says He, "when I am gone, where shall you find the great infallible teacher? Shall I set you up a Pope at Rome, to whom you shall go, and who shall be your infallible oracle? Shall I give you the councils of the church to be held to decide all knotty points?" Christ said no such thing. "I am the infallible paraclete or teacher, and when I am gone, I will send you another teacher and He shall be the person who is to explain Scripture; He shall be the authoritative oracle of God, who shall make all dark things light, who shall unravel mysteries, who shall untwist all knots of revelation, and shall make you understand what you could not discover, had it not been for His influence."

And beloved, no man ever learns anything aright, unless he is taught of the Spirit. No man can know Jesus Christ unless he is taught of God. There is no doctrine of the Bible which can be safely, thoroughly, and truly learned, except by the agency of the one authoritative teacher. Ah! tell me not of systems of divinity; tell me not of schemes of theology; tell me not of infallible commentators, or most learned and most arrogant doctors; but tell me of the Great Teacher, who shall instruct us, the sons of God, and shall make us wise to understand all things. He is *the* Teacher; it matters not what this or that man says; I rest on no man's boasting authority, nor will you. Ye are not to be carried away with the craftiness of men, nor sleight of words, this is the authoritative oracle, the Holy Ghost resting in the hearts of His children.

The other translation is *Advocate*. Have you ever thought how the Holy Ghost can be said to be an advocate? You know Jesus Christ is called the wonderful, the counsellor, and mighty God; but how can the Holy Ghost be said to be an advocate? I suppose it is thus: He is an advocate on earth to plead against the enemies of the cross. How was it that Paul could so ably plead before Felix and Agrippa? How was it that the Apostles stood unawed before the magistrates and confessed their Lord? How has it come to pass that in all times God's ministers have been made fearless as lions, and their brows have been firmer than brass, their hearts sterner than steel, and their words like the language of God? Why, it is simply for this reason, that it was not the man who pleaded, but it was God the Holy Ghost pleading through him.

But, besides this, the Holy Ghost is the advocate in men's hearts. Ah! I have known men reject a doctrine until the Holy Ghost began to illumine them. We who are the advocates of the truth are often very poor pleaders; we spoil our cause by the words we use; but it is a mercy that the brief is in the hand of a special pleader, who will advocate successfully and overcome the sinner's opposition. Did you ever know Him fail once? Brethren, I speak to your souls: has not God in old times convinced you of sin? Did not the Holy Ghost come and prove that you were guilty, although no minister could ever get you out of your self-righteousness? Did He not advocate Christ's righteousness? Did He not stand and tell you that your works were filthy rags? and did He not convince you of the judgment to come? He is a mighty advocate when He pleads in the soul—of sin, of righteousness, and of the judgment to come. Blessed advocate! plead in my heart, plead with my conscience. When I sin, make conscience bold to tell me of it; when I err, make conscience speak at once; and when I turn aside to crooked ways, then advocate the cause of righteousness, and bid me sit down in confusion, knowing my guiltiness in the sight of God.

But there is yet another sense in which the Holy Ghost advocates, and that is, He advocates our cause with Jesus Christ, with groanings that cannot be uttered. O my soul, thou art ready to burst within me! O my heart, thou art swelled with grief; the hot tide of my emotion would well-nigh overflow the channels of my veins. I long to speak, but the very desire chains my tongue. I wish to pray, but the fervency of my feeling curbs my language. There is a groaning within that cannot be uttered. Do you know who can utter that groaning, who can understand it, and who can put it into heavenly language and utter it in a celestial tongue, so that Christ can hear it? Oh! yes; it is God the Holy Spirit; He advocates our cause with Christ, and then Christ advocates it with His Father. He is the advocate, who maketh intercession for us, with groanings that cannot be uttered.

Having thus explained the Spirit's office as teacher and advocate, we come now to the translation of our version—the *Comforter ;* and here I shall have three divisions. First, the *comforter ;* secondly, the *comfort ;* and thirdly, the *comforted*.

I. First, then, the COMFORTER. Briefly let me run over in my mind and in your minds, too, the characteristics of this glorious Comforter. Let me tell you some of the attributes of His comfort, so that you may understand how well adapted He is to your case.

And first, we will remark that God the Holy Ghost is a very *loving* Comforter. I am in distress and want consolation. Some passer-by hears of my sorrow, and he steps within, sits down and essays to cheer me; he speaks soothing words; but he loves me not, he is a stranger, he knows me not at all, he has only come in to try his skill; and what is the consequence? his words run o'er me like oil upon a slab of marble—they are like the pattering rain upon the rock; they do not break my grief; it stands unmoved as adamant, because he has no love for me. But let some one who loves me dearly as his own life come and plead with me, then truly his words are music; they taste like honey; he knows the pass-word of the doors of my heart, and my ear is attentive to every word; I catch the intonation of each syllable as it falls, for it is like the harmony of the harps of heaven. Oh! there is a voice in love, it speaks a language which is its own, it is an idiom and an accent which none can mimic; wisdom cannot imitate it; oratory cannot attain unto it; it is love alone which can reach the mourning heart; love is the only handkerchief which can wipe the mourner's tears away.

And is not the Holy Ghost a loving Comforter? Dost thou know, O saint, how much the Holy Spirit loves thee? Canst thou measure the love of the Spirit? Dost thou know how great is the affection of His soul towards thee? Go, measure heaven with thy span; go, weigh the mountains in the scales; go, take the ocean's water, and tell each drop; go, count the sand upon the sea's wide shore; and when thou hast accomplished this, thou canst tell how much He loveth thee. He has loved thee long; He has loved thee well; He loved thee ever; and He still shall love thee. Surely He is the person to comfort thee, because He loves. Admit Him, then, to your heart, O Christian, that He may comfort you in your distress.

But next He is a *faithful* Comforter. Love sometimes proveth unfaithful. "Oh! sharper than a serpent's tooth" is an unfaithful friend! Oh! far more bitter than the gall of bitterness, to have a friend to turn from me in my distress! Oh! woe of woes, to have one who loves me in my prosperity forsake me in the dark day of my trouble. Sad indeed: but such is not God's Spirit. He ever loves, and loves even to the end—a faithful Comforter. Child of God, you are in trouble. A little while ago you found Him a sweet and loving Comforter; you obtained relief from Him when others were but broken cisterns; He sheltered you in His bosom, and carried you in His arms. Oh, wherefore dost thou distrust Him now? Away with thy fears! for He is a faithful Comforter. "Ah! but," thou sayest, "I have sinned." So thou hast, but sin cannot sever thee from His love; He loves thee still. Think not, O poor downcast child of God, because the scars of thine old sins have marred thy beauty, that He loves thee less because of that blemish. Oh, no! He loved thee when He foreknew thy sin; He loved thee with the knowledge of what the aggregate of thy wickedness would be; and He does not love thee less now. Come to Him in all boldness of faith; tell Him thou hast grieved Him, and He will forget thy wandering, and will receive thee again; the kisses of His love shall be bestowed upon thee, and the arms of His grace shall embrace thee. He is faithful: trust Him; He will never deceive you; trust Him, He will never leave you.

And oh, how *wise* a Comforter is the Holy Ghost. Job had comforters, and I think he spoke the truth when he said, "Miserable comforters are ye all." But I dare say they esteemed themselves wise; and when the young man Elihu rose to speak, they thought he had a world of impudence. Were they not "grave and reverend seniors?" Did not they comprehend his grief and sorrow? If they could not comfort him, who could? But they did not find out the cause. They thought he was not really a child of God, that he was self-righteous; and they gave him the wrong physic. It is a bad case when the doctor mistakes the disease and gives a wrong prescription, and so, perhaps, kills the patient. Sometimes, when we go and visit people we mistake their disease, we want to comfort them on this point, whereas they do not require any such comfort at all, and they would be better left alone than spoiled by such unwise comforters as we are. But oh! how wise the Holy Spirit is! He takes the soul, lays it on the table, and dissects it in a moment; He finds out the root of the matter, He sees where the complaint is, and then He applies the knife where something is required to be taken away, or puts a plaster where the sore is; and He never mistakes. Oh! how wise, the blessed Holy Ghost! from every comforter I turn and leave them all, for thou art He who alone givest the wisest consolation.

Then mark how *safe* a Comforter the Holy Ghost is. All comfort is not safe; mark that. There is a young man over there very melancholy. You know how he became so. He stepped into the house of God and heard a powerful preacher, and the word was blessed and convinced him of sin. When he went home, his father and the rest found there was something different about him, "Oh," they said, "John is mad; he is crazy"; and what said his mother? "Send him into the country for a week; let him go to the ball or to the theatre." John! Did you find any comfort there? "Ah, no; they made me worse, for while I was there, I thought hell might open and swallow me up." Did you find any relief in the gaieties of the world? "No," say you, "I thought it was idle waste of time." Alas! this is miserable comfort, but it is the comfort of the worldling; and when a Christian gets into distress, how many will recommend him this remedy and the other. Ah, there have been many, like infants, destroyed by elixirs given to lull them to sleep; many have been ruined by the cry of "peace, peace," when there is no peace, hearing gentle things when they ought to be stirred to the quick. Cleopatra's asp was brought in a basket of flowers; and men's ruin often lurks in fair and sweet speeches. But the Holy Ghost's comfort is safe, and you may rest on it. Let Him speak the word, and there is a reality about it; let Him give the cup of consolation, and you may drink it to the bottom, for in its depths there are no dregs, nothing to intoxicate or ruin, it is all safe.

Moreover, the Holy Ghost is an *active* Comforter: He does not comfort by words, but by deeds. Some comfort by "Be ye warmed and be ye filled," giving nothing. But the Holy Ghost gives, He intercedes with Jesus, He gives us promises, He gives us grace, and so He comforts us. Mark again, He is always a *successful* Comforter; He never attempts what He cannot accomplish.

Then to close up, He is an *ever-present* Comforter, so that you never have to send for Him. Your God is always near you, and when you need comfort in your distress, behold, the word is nigh thee, it is in thy mouth, and in thy heart; He is an ever-present help in time of trouble.

II. The second thing is the COMFORT. Now there are some persons who make a great mistake about the influence of the Holy Spirit. A foolish man, who had a fancy to preach in a certain pulpit, though in truth he was quite incapable of the duty, called upon the minister, and assured him solemnly that it had been revealed to him by the Holy Ghost, that he was to preach in his pulpit. "Very well," said the minister, "I suppose I must not doubt your assertion, but as it has not been revealed to me that I am to let you preach, you must go your way until it is." I have heard many fanatical persons say the Holy Spirit revealed this and that to them. Now that is very generally revealed nonsense. The Holy Ghost does not reveal anything fresh now. He brings old things to our remembrance. "He shall teach you all things, and bring all things to your remembrance whatsoever I have told you." The canon of revelation is closed; there is no more to be added. God does not give a fresh revelation, but He rivets the old one. When it has been forgotten, and laid in the dusty chamber of our memory, He fetches it out and cleans the picture, but does not paint a new one. There are no new doctrines, but the old ones are often revived. It is not, I say, by any new revelation that the Spirit comforts. He does so by telling us old things over again; He brings a fresh lamp to manifest the treasures hidden in Scripture; He unlocks the strong chests in which the truth had long lain, and He points to secret chambers filled with untold riches; but He coins no more, for enough is done. Believer! there is enough in the Bible for thee to live upon for ever. If thou shouldst outnumber the years of Methusaleh, there would be no need for a fresh revelation; if thou shouldst live till Christ should come upon the earth, there would be no necessity for the addition of a single word; if thou shouldst go down as deep as Jonah, or even descend as David said he did, into the belly of hell, still there would be enough in the Bible to comfort thee without a supplementary sentence. But Christ says, "He shall take of mine and shall show it unto you." Now let me just tell you briefly what it is the Holy Ghost tells us.

Ah! does He not whisper to the heart, "Saint, be of good cheer; there is one who died for thee; look to Calvary; behold His wounds; see the torrent gushing from His side; there is thy purchaser, and thou art secure. He loves thee with an everlasting love, and this chastisement is meant for thy good; each stroke is working thy healing; by the blueness of the wound thy soul is made better.

B

"Whom he loveth he chasteneth, and scourgeth every son whom he receiveth." Doubt not His grace, because of thy tribulation, but believe that He loveth thee as much in seasons of trouble as in times of happiness." And then, moreover, He says, "What is all thy suffering compared with that of thy Lord's? or what, when weighed in the scales of Jesu's agonies, is all thy distress?" And especially at times does the Holy Ghost take back the veil of heaven, and lets the soul behold the glory of the upper world! then it is that the saint can say, "Oh, thou art a Comforter to me!"

> " Let cares like a wild deluge come,
>   And storms of sorrow fall;
> May I but safely reach my home,
>   My God, my heaven, my all."

Some of you could follow, were I to tell of manifestations of heaven. You too have left sun, moon, and stars, at your feet, while in your flight, outstripping the tardy lightning, you have seemed to enter the gates of pearl, and tread the golden streets, borne aloft on wings of the Spirit. But here we must not trust ourselves, lest, lost in reverie, we forget our theme.

III. And now thirdly, who are the COMFORTED persons? I like, you know, at the end of my sermon to cry out "Divide! divide!" There are two parties here—some who are the comforted, and others who are the comfortless ones—some who have received the consolation of the Holy Ghost, and some who have not. Now let us try and sift you, and see which is the chaff, and which is the wheat; and may God grant that some of the chaff may this night be transformed into His wheat.

You may say, "How am I to know whether I am a recipient of the comfort of the Holy Ghost?" You may know it by one rule. If you have received one blessing from God, you will receive all other blessings too. Let me explain myself. If I could come here as an auctioneer, and sell the gospel off in lots, I should dispose of it all. If I could say here is justification through the blood of Christ, free, given away, gratis; many a one would say, "I will have justification: give it me; I wish to be justified, I wish to be pardoned." Suppose I took sanctification, the giving up of all sin, a thorough change of heart, leaving off drunkenness and swearing, many would say, "I don't want that; I should like to go to heaven, but I do not want that holiness; I should like to be saved at last, but I should like to have my drink still; I should like to enter glory, but then I must have an oath or two on the road." Nay, but sinner, if thou hast one blessing, thou shalt have all. God will never divide the gospel. He will not give justification to that man, and sanctification to another; pardon to one and holiness to another. No, it all goes together. Whom He calls then He justifies; whom He justifies, then He sanctifies; and whom He sanctifies, them He also glorifies.

Oh; if I could lay down nothing but the *comforts* of the gospel, ye would fly to them as flies do to honey. When ye come to be ill, ye send for the clergyman. Ah! you all want your minister then to come and give you consoling words. But if he be an honest man, he will not give some of you a particle of consolation. He will not commence pouring oil when the knife would be better. I want to make a man feel his sins before I dare tell him anything about Christ. I want to probe into his soul and make him feel that he is lost before I tell him anything about the purchased blessing. Have you had conviction of sin? Have you ever felt your guilt before God? Have your souls been humbled at Jesus' feet? And have you been made to look to Calvary alone for your refuge? If not, you have no right to consolation. Do not take an atom of it. The Spirit is a Convincer before He is a Comforter; and you must have the other operations of the Holy Spirit before you can derive anything from this.

And now I have done. You have heard what this babbler hath said once more. What has it been? Something about the Comforter. But let me ask you, before you go, what do you know about the Comforter? Each one of you before descending the steps of this chapel, let this solemn question thrill through your souls—What do you know of the Comforter? Oh! poor souls, if ye know not the Comforter, I will tell you what you shall know —You shall know the Judge! If ye know not the Comforter on earth, ye shall know the Condemner in the next world, who shall cry, "Depart ye cursed into everlasting fire in hell." Well might Whitfield call out, "O earth, earth, earth, hear the Word of the Lord!" If we were to live here for ever, ye might slight the gospel; if ye had a lease of your lives, ye might despise the Comforter. But sirs, ye must die. Since last we met together, probably some have gone to their long last home; and ere we meet again in this sanctuary, some here will be amongst the glorified above, or amongst the damned below. Which will it be? Let your soul answer. If to-night you fell down dead in your pews, or where you are standing in the gallery, where would you be? in *heaven* or in *hell*?

Ah! deceive not yourselves; let conscience have its perfect work; and if, in the sight of God, you are obliged to say, "I tremble and fear lest my portion should be with unbelievers," listen one moment, and then I have done with thee. "He that believeth and is baptized shall be saved, and he that believeth not shall be damned." Weary sinner, thou who art the devil's casta- way, reprobate, profligate, harlot, robber, thief, adulterer,

fornicator, drunkard, swearer, Sabbath-breaker—list! I speak
to thee as well as the rest. I exempt no man. God hath said there
is no exemption here. "*Whosoever* believeth in the name of
Jesus Christ shall be saved." Sin is no barrier: thy guilt is no
obstacle. Whosoever—though he were as black as Satan, though
he were filthy as a fiend—whosoever this night believes, shall
have every sin forgiven, shall have every crime effaced, shall
have every iniquity blotted out; shall be saved in the Lord Jesus
Christ, and shall stand in heaven safe and secure. That is the
glorious gospel. God apply it home to your hearts, and give you
faith in Jesus!

> " We have listened to the preacher—
>   Truth by him has now been shown;
> But we want a GREATER TEACHER,
>   From the everlasting throne:
>   APPLICATION
>   Is the work of God *alone*."

THE POWER OF THE HOLY GHOST

A Sermon

Text.—"The power of the Holy Ghost."—Rom. xv. 13.

POWER is the special and peculiar prerogative of God, and God alone. "Twice have I have heard this: that power belongeth unto God." God is God: and power belongeth to him. If He delegates a portion of it to His creatures, yet still it is *His* power. The sun, although he is "like a bridegroom coming out of his chamber, and rejoiceth as a strong man to run his race," yet has no power to perform his motions except as God directs him. The stars, although they travel in their orbits and none could stay them, yet have neither might nor force except that which God daily infuses into them. The tall archangel, near His throne, who outshines a comet in its blaze, though he is one of those who excel in strength and hearken to the voice of the commands of God, yet has no might except that which his Maker gives to him. As for Leviathan, who so maketh the sea to boil like a pot that one would think the deep were hoary: as for Behemoth, who drinketh up Jordan at a draught, and boasteth that he can snuff up rivers; as for those majestic creatures that are found on earth, they owe their strength to Him who fashioned their bones of steel and made their sinews of brass. And when we think of man, if he has might or power, it is so small and insignificant, that we can scarcely call it such; yea, when it is at its greatest—when he sways his sceptre, when he commands hosts, when he rules nations—still the power belongeth unto God; and it is true, "Twice have I heard this, that power belongeth unto God."

This exclusive prerogative of God, is to be found in each of the three persons of the glorious Trinity. The Father hath power: for by His word were the heavens made, and all the host of them ; by His strength all things stand, and through Him they fulfil their destiny. The Son hath power: for like His Father, He is the Creator of all things; "Without Him was not anything made that was made," and "by him all things consist." And the Holy Spirit hath power. It is concerning the power of the Holy Ghost that I shall speak this morning; and may you have a practical exemplification of that attribute in your own hearts, when you shall feel that the influence of the Holy Ghost is being poured out upon me, so that I am speaking the words of the living God to your souls, and bestowed upon you when you are feeling the effects of it in your own spirits.

We shall look at the power of the Holy Ghost in three ways this morning. First, *the outward and visible displays of it ;* second, *the inward and spiritual manifestations of it ;* and third, *the future and expected works thereof.* The power of the Spirit will thus, I trust, be made clearly present to your souls.

I. First, then, we are to view the power of the Spirit in the OUTWARD AND VISIBLE DISPLAYS OF IT. The power of the Spirit has not been dormant; it has exerted itself. Much has been done by the Spirit of God already; more than could have been accomplished by any being except the Infinite, Eternal, Almighty Jehovah, of whom the Holy Spirit is one person. There are four works which are the outward and manifest signs of the power of the Spirit: creation works; resurrection works; works of attestation, or of witness; and works of grace. Of each of the works I shall speak very briefly.

1. First, the Spirit has manifested the omnipotence of His power in *creation works;* for though not very frequently in Scripture, yet sometimes creation is ascribed to the Holy Ghost, as well as to the Father and the Son. The creation of the heavens above us is said to be the work of God's Spirit. This you will see at once by referring to the sacred Scriptures, Job xxvi. 13th verse, "By his Spirit he hath garnished the heavens; his hand hath formed the crooked serpent." All the stars of heaven are said to have been placed aloft by the Spirit, and one particular constellation called the "crooked serpent" is specially pointed out as His handiwork. He looseth the bands of Orion; He bindeth the sweet influences of the Pleiades, and guides Acturus with his sons. He made all those stars that shine in heaven. The heavens were garnished by His hands, and He formed the crooked serpent by His might. So also in those continued acts of creation which are still performed in the world; as the bringing forth of man and animals, their birth and generation. These are ascribed also to the Holy Ghost. If you look at the 104th Psalm, at the 29th verse, you will read, "Thou hidest thy face, they are troubled: thou takest away their breath, they die, and return to their dust. Thou sendest forth thy Spirit, they are created: and thou renewest the face of the earth." So that the creation of every man is the work of the Spirit: and the creation of all life and all flesh-existence in this work is as much to be ascribed to the power of the Spirit as the first garnishing of the heavens, or the fashioning of the crooked serpent.

But if you will look in the 1st chapter of Genesis, you will there see more particularly set forth that peculiar operation of power upon the universe which was put forth by the Holy Spirit; you will then discover what was His special work. In the 2nd verse of the 1st chapter of Genesis, we read, "And the earth was without form, and void; and darkness was upon the face of the deep. And the spirit of God moved upon the face of the waters."

We know not how remote the period of the creation of this globe may be—certainly many millions of years before the time of Adam. Our planet has passed through various stages of existence, and different kinds of creatures have lived on its surface, all of which have been fashioned by God. But before that era came, wherein man should be its principal tenant and monarch, the Creator gave up the world to confusion. He allowed the inward fires to burst up from beneath and melt all the solid matter, so that all kinds of substances were commingled in one vast mass of disorder; the only name you could give to the world then was, that it was a chaotic mass of matter; what it should be, you could not guess or define. It was entirely without form, and void; and darkness was upon the face of the deep. The Spirit came, and stretching His broad wings, bade the darkness disperse, and as He moved over it, all the different portions of matter came into their places, and it was no longer "without form, and void"; but became round like its sister planets, and moved, singing the high praises of God—not discordantly as it had done before, but as one great note in the vast scale of creation.

But there was one particular instance of creation in which the Holy Spirit was more especially concerned; viz., the formation of the body of our Lord Jesus Christ. Though our Lord Jesus Christ was born of a woman and made in the likeness of sinful flesh, yet the power that begat Him was entirely in God the Holy Spirit—as the Scriptures express it, "The power of the Highest shall overshadow thee." He was begotten as the Apostles' Creed says, begotten of the Holy Ghost. "That holy thing which is born of thee shall be called the Son of the Highest." The corporeal frame of the Lord Jesus Christ was a masterpiece of the Holy Spirit. I suppose His body to have excelled all others in beauty; to have been like that of the first man, the very pattern of what the body is to be in heaven, when it shall shine forth in all its glory. That fabric, in all its beauty and perfection, was modelled by the Spirit. In His book were all the members written when as yet there were none of them. He fashioned and formed Him; and here again we have another instance of the creative energy of the Spirit.

2. A second manifestation of the Holy Spirit's power is to be found in the *resurrection of the Lord Jesus Christ*. If ye have ever studied this subject, ye have perhaps been rather perplexed to find that sometimes the resurrection of Christ is ascribed to Himself. By His own power and Godhead He could not be held by the bond of death, but as He willingly gave up His life He had power to take it again. In another portion of Scripture you find it ascribed to God the Father: "He raised him up from the dead": "Him hath God the Father exalted." And many other

passages of similar import. But, again, it is said in Scripture that Jesus Christ was raised by the Holy Spirit. Now all these things were true. He was raised by the Father because the Father said, "Loose the prisoner—let him go. Justice is satisfied. My law requires no more satisfaction—vengeance has had its due—let him go." Here He gave an official message which delivered Jesus from the grave. He was raised by His own majesty and power because He had a right to come out; and He felt He had, and therefore "burst the bonds of death: he could be no longer holden of them." But, He was raised by the Spirit as to that energy which His mortal frame received, by the which it rose again from the grave after having lain there for three days and nights. If you want proofs of this you must open your Bibles again, 1 Peter, iii. 18. "For Christ also hath once suffered for sins, the just for the unjust, that he might bring us to God, being put to death in the flesh but quickened by the Spirit." And a further proof you may find in Romans, viii. 11. "But if the Spirit of him that raised up Jesus from the dead dwell in you, he that raised up Christ from the dead shall also quicken your mortal bodies by his Spirit that dwelleth in you."

The resurrection of Christ, then, was effected by the agency of the Spirit; and here we have a noble illustration of His omnipotence. Could you have stepped, as angels did, into the grave of Jesus, and seen His sleeping body, you would have found it cold as any other corpse. Lift up the hand; it falls by the side. Look at the eye: it is glazed. And there is a death-thrust which must have annihilated life. See His hands: the blood distils not from them. They are cold and motionless. Can that body live? Can it start up? Yes; and be an illustration of the might of the Spirit. For when the power of the Spirit came on Him, as it was when it fell upon the dry bones of the valley: "he arose in the majesty of his divinity, and bright and shining, astonished the watchmen so that they fled away; yea, he rose no more to die, but to live for ever, King of kings and Prince of the kings of the earth."

3. The third of the works of the Holy Spirit which have so wonderfully demonstrated His power, are *attestation works*. I mean by this,—works of witnessing. When Jesus Christ went into the stream of baptism in the river Jordan, the Holy Spirit descended upon Him like a dove, and proclaimed Him God's beloved son. That was what I style an attestation work. And when afterwards Jesus Christ raised the dead, when He healed the leper, when He spoke to diseases and they fled apace, when demons rushed in thousands from those who were possessed of them, it was done by the power of the Spirit. The Spirit dwelt in Jesus without measure, and by that power all those miracles

were worked. These were attestation works. And when Jesus Christ was gone, you will remember that master attestation of the Spirit when He came like a rushing mighty wind upon the assembled apostles, and cloven tongues sat upon them; and you will remember how He attested their ministry by giving them to speak with tongues as He gave them utterance; and how, also, miraculous deeds were wrought by them, how they taught, how Peter raised Dorcas, how He breathed life into Eutycus, how great deeds were wrought by the apostles as well as their Master—so that "mighty signs and wonders were done by the Holy Ghost, and many believed thereby." Who will doubt the power of the Holy Spirit after that? Ah! those Socinians who deny the existence of the Holy Ghost and His absolute personality, what will they do when we get them on creation, resurrection, and attestation? They must rush in the very teeth of Scripture. But mark! it is a stone upon which if any man fall he shall be bruised; but if it fall upon him, as it will do if he resists it, it shall grind him to powder. The Holy Spirit has power omnipotent, even the power of God.

4. Once more, if we want another outward and visible sign of the power of the Spirit, we may look at the *works of grace*. Behold a city where a soothsayer hath the power—who has given out himself to be some great one, a Philip enters it and preaches the Word of God, straightway a Simon Magus loses his power and himself seeks for the power of the Spirit to be given to him, fancying it might be purchased with money. See, in modern times, a country where the inhabitants live in miserable wigwams, feeding on reptiles and the meanest creatures; observe them bowing down before their idols and worshipping their false gods, and so plunged in superstition, so degraded and debased, that it became a question whether they had souls or not; behold a Moffat go with the Word of God in his hand, hear him preach as the Spirit gives him utterance, and accompanies that Word with power. They cast aside their idols—they hate and abhor their former lusts; they build houses, wherein they dwell; they become clothed, and in their right mind. They break the bow, and cut the spear in sunder; the uncivilized become civilized; the savage becomes polite; he who knew nothing begins to read the Scripture; thus out of the mouths of Hottentots God attests the power of His mighty Spirit

Take a household in this city—and we could guide you to many such—the father is a drunkard; he has been the most desperate of characters; see him in his madness, and you might just as well meet an unchained tiger as meet such a man. He seems as if he could rend a man to pieces who should offend him. Mark his wife. She, too, has a spirit in her, and when he treats her ill she can resist him; many broils have been seen in that house, and often has the neighbourhood been disturbed by the noise created there. As for the poor little children—see them in their rags and nakedness, poor untaught things. Untaught, did I say? They are taught and well taught in the devil's school, and are growing up to be the heirs of damnation. But some one whom God has blessed by His Spirit is guided to the house. He may be but a humble city missionary perhaps, but he speaks to such a one: O, says he, come and listen to the voice of God. Whether it is by His own agency, or a minister's preaching, the Word, which is quick and powerful, cuts to the sinner's heart. The tears run down his cheeks—such as had never been seen before. He shakes and quivers. The strong man bows down—the mighty man trembles—and those knees that never shook begin to knock together. That heart which never quailed before, now begins to shake before the power of the Spirit. He sits down on a humble bench by the penitent; he lets his knees bend, whilst his lips utter a child's prayer, but, whilst a child's prayer, a prayer of a child of God. He becomes a changed character. Mark the reformation in his house! That wife of his becomes the decent matron. Those children are the credit of the house, and in due time they grow up like olive branches round his table, adorning his house like polished stones. Pass by the house—no noise or broils, but songs of Zion. See him—no drunken revelry; he has drained his last cup; and, now forswearing it, he comes to God and is His servant. Now, you will not hear at midnight the bacchanalian shout; but should there be a noise, it will be the sound of the solemn hymn of praise to God. And, now, is there not such a thing as the power of the Spirit? Yes! and these must have witnessed it, and seen it.

I know a village, once, perhaps, the most profane in England—a village inundated by drunkenness and debauchery of the worst kind, where it was impossible almost for an honest traveller to stop in the public house without being annoyed by blasphemy; a place noted for incendiaries and robbers. One man, the ringleader of all, listened to the voice of God. That man's heart was broken. The whole gang came to hear the gospel preached, and they sat and seemed to reverence the preacher as if he were a God, and not a man. These men became changed and reformed; and every one who knows the place affirms that such a change had never been wrought but by the power of the Holy Ghost. Let the gospel be preached and the Spirit poured out, and you will see that it has such power to change the conscience, to ameliorate the conduct, to raise the debased, to chastise and to curb the wickedness of the race, that you must glory in it. I say, there is nought like the power of the Spirit. Only let that come, and, indeed, everything can be accomplished.

II. Now, for the second point, THE INWARD AND SPIRITUAL POWER OF THE HOLY SPIRIT. What I have already spoken of may be seen; what I am about to speak of must be felt, and no man will apprehend what I say with truth unless he has felt it.

1. First, in that the Holy Ghost has *a power over men's hearts*. Now, men's hearts are very hard to affect. If you want to get them for any worldly object you can do it. A cheating world can win man's heart; a little gold can win man's heart; a trump of fame and a little clamour of applause can win man's heart. But there is a not a minister breathing that can win man's heart himself. He can win his ears and make them listen; he can win his eyes and fix those eyes upon him; he can win the attention, but the heart is very slippery. Yes, the heart is a fish that troubles all gospel fishermen to hold. You may sometimes pull it almost all out of the water; but slimy as an eel, it slippeth between your fingers, and you have not captured it after all. Many a man has fancied that he has caught the heart but has been disappointed. It would need a strong hunter to overtake the hart on the mountains. It is too fleet for human foot to approach.

The Spirit alone has power over man's heart. Do you ever try your power on a heart? If any man thinks that a minister can convert the soul, I wish he would try. Let him go and be a Sabbath-school teacher. He shall take his class, he shall have the best books that can be obtained, he shall have the best rules, he shall draw his lines of circumvallation about his spiritual Sebastopol, he shall take the best boy in his class, and if he is not tired in a week I shall be very much mistaken. Let him spend four or five Sabbaths in trying, but he will say, "The young fellow is incorrigible." Let him try another. And he will have to try another, and another, and another, before he will manage to convert one. He will soon find "It is not by might nor by power, but by my Spirit, saith the Lord." We cannot reach the soul; but the Holy Spirit can. "My beloved can put in his hand by the hole in the door and my bowels will move for sin." He can give a sense of blood-bought pardon that shall dissolve a heart of stone. He can

> " Speak with that voice which wakes the dead,
>   And bids the sinner rise:
>   And makes the guilty conscience dread
>   The death that never dies."

He can make Sinai's thunders audible; yea, and He can make the sweet whisperings of Calvary enter into the soul. He has power over the heart of man. And here is a glorious proof of the omnipotence of the Spirit that He has rule over the heart.

2. But if there is one thing more stubborn than the heart it is *the will*. "My lord Will-be-will," as Bunyan calls him in his "Holy War," is a fellow who will not easily be bent. The will, especially in some men, is a very stubborn thing, and in all men, if the will is once stirred up to opposition, there is nothing can be done with them. *Freewill* somebody believes in. *Freewill* many dream of. Freewill! wherever is that to be found? Once there was freewill in Paradise, and a terrible mess freewill made there, for it all spoiled all Paradise and turned Adam out of the garden. Freewill was once in heaven; but it turned the glorious archangel out, and a third part of the stars of heaven fell into the abyss. Yet some boast of freewill. I wonder whether those who believe in it have any more power over persons' wills than I have. I know I have not any. I find the old proverb very true, "One man can bring a horse to the water, but a hundred cannot make him drink." I do not think any man has power over his fellow-creature's will, but the Spirit of God has. "I will make them willing in the day of my power." He maketh the unwilling sinner so willing that he is impetuous after the gospel; he who was obstinate, now hurries to the cross. He who laughed at Jesus, now hands on His mercy; and he who would not believe, is now made by the Holy Spirit to do it, not only willingly, but eagerly; he is happy, is glad to do it, rejoices in the sound of Jesus's name, and delights to run in the way of God's commandments. The Holy Spirit has power over the will.

3. And yet there is one thing more which I think is rather worse than the will. You will guess what I mean. The will is somewhat worse than the heart to bend, but there is one thing that excels the will in its naughtiness, and that is the *imagination*. I hope that my will is managed by Divine Grace. But I am afraid my imagination is not at times. Those who have a fair share of imagination know what a difficult thing it is to control. You cannot restrain it. It will break the reins. You will never be able to manage it. The imagination will sometimes fly up to God with such a power that eagles' wings cannot match it. It sometimes has such might that it can almost see the King in His beauty, and the land which is very far off. With regard to myself, my imagination will sometimes take me over the gates of iron, across that infinite unknown, to the very gates of pearl, and discovers the blessed glorified.

But if it is potent one way it is another; for my imagination has taken me down to the vilest kennels and sewers of earth. It has given me thoughts so dreadful, that while I could not avoid them, yet I was thoroughly horrified at them. These thoughts will come; and when I feel in the holiest frame, the most devoted to God, and the most earnest in prayer, it often happens that that is the very time when the plagues break out the worst. But I rejoice and think of one thing, that I can cry out when this imagination comes upon me. I know it is said in the Book of Leviticus, when an act of evil was committed, if the maiden cried out against it, then her life was to be spared. So it is with the Christian. If he cries out, there is hope. Can you chain your imagination? No; but the power of the Holy Ghost can. Ah, it shall do it, and it does do it at last; it does it even on earth.

III. But the last thing was, THE FUTURE AND DESIRED EFFECTS; for after all, though the Holy Spirit has done so much, He cannot say, "It is finished." Jesus Christ could exclaim concerning His own labour—"It is finished." But the Holy Spirit cannot say that. He has more to do yet: and until the consummation of all things, when the Son Himself becomes subject to the Father, it shall not be said by the Holy Spirit, "It is finished." What, then, has the Holy Spirit to do?

1. First, He has to *perfect us in holiness.* There are two kinds of perfection which a Christian needs—one is the perfection of justification in the person of Jesus; and the other is, the perfection of sanctification worked in him by the Holy Spirit. At present corruption still rests even in the breasts of the regenerate. At present the heart is partially impure. At present there are still lusts and evil imaginations. But, oh! my soul rejoices to know that the day is coming when God shall finish the work which He has begun; and He shall present my soul, not only perfect in Christ, but, perfect in the Spirit, without spot or blemish, or any such thing. And is it true that this poor depraved heart is to become as holy as that of God? And is it true that this poor spirit, which often cries, "O wretched man that I am, who shall deliver me from the body of this sin and death!" shall get rid of sin and death—I shall have no evil things to vex my ears, and no unholy thoughts to disturb my peace? Oh! happy hour! Oh! to be washed white, clean, pure, perfect! Not an angel more pure than I shall be—yea, not God Himself more holy! And I shall be able to say, in a double sense, "Great God, I am clean— through Jesus's blood I am clean, through the Spirit's work I am clean too!" Must we not extol the power of the Holy Ghost in thus making us fit to stand before our Father in heaven?

2. Another great work of the Holy Spirit which is not accomplished is *the bringing on of the latter-day glory.* In a few more years— I know not when, I know not how—the Holy Spirit will be poured out in a far different style from the present. There are diversities of operations; and during the last few years it has been the case that the diversified operations have consisted in very little pouring out of the Spirit. Ministers have gone on in dull routine,

continually preaching—preaching—preaching, and little good has been done. But the hour is coming when the Holy Ghost shall be poured out again in such a wonderful manner that many shall run to and fro, and knowledge shall be increased—the knowledge of the Lord shall cover the earth as the waters cover the surface of the great deep; when His kingdom shall come, and His will shall be done on earth even as it is in heaven. We are not going to be dragging on for ever like Pharaoh with the wheels off his chariot. Perhaps there shall be no miraculous gifts—for they will not be required; but yet there shall be such a miraculous amount of holiness, such an extraordinary fervour of prayer, such a real communion with God and so much vital religion, and such a spread of the doctrines of the cross, that every one will see that verily the Spirit is poured out like water, and the rains are descending from above. For that let us pray: let us continually labour for it, and seek it of God.

3. One more work of the Spirit which will especially manifest His power—*the general resurrection*. We have reason to believe from Scripture that the resurrection of the dead, whilst it will be effected by the voice of God and of His Word (the Son) shall also be brought about by the Spirit. That same power which raised Jesus Christ from the dead, shall also quicken your mortal bodies. The power of the resurrection is perhaps one of the finest proofs of the works of the Spirit. Ah! my friends, if this earth could but have its mantle torn away for a little while, if the green sod could be cut from it, and we could look about six feet deep into its bowels, what a world it would seem! What should we see? Bones, carcasses, rottenness, worms, corruption. And you would say, "Can these dry bones live? Can they start up?" "Yes! in a moment! in the twinkling of an eye, at the last trump, the dead shall be raised." He speaks: they are alive! See them scattered: bone comes to his bone! See them naked: flesh comes upon them! See them still lifeless: "Come from the four winds, O breath, and breathe upon these slain!" When the wind of the Holy Spirit comes, they live, and they stand upon their feet an exceeding great army.

I have thus attempted to speak of the power of the Spirit, and I trust I have shewn it to you. We must now have a moment or two for practical inference. The Spirit is very powerful, Christian! What do you infer from that fact? Why, that you never need distrust the power of God to carry you to heaven. O how that sweet verse was laid to my soul yesterday!

> "His tried Almighty arm
>   Is raised for your defence;
>   Where is the power can reach you there?
>   Or what can pluck you thence?"

The power of the Holy Spirit is your bulwark, and all His omnipotence defends you. Can your enemies overcome omnipotence? then they can conquer you. Can they wrestle with Deity, and hurl Him to the ground? then they might conquer you. For the power of the Spirit is our power; the power of the Spirit is our might.

Once again, Christians, if this is the power of the Spirit, *why should you doubt anything?* There is your son. There is that wife of yours for whom you have supplicated so frequently: do not doubt the Spirit's power. "Though he tarry, wait for him." There is thy husband, O holy woman! and thou hast wrestled for his soul. And though he is ever so hardened and desperate a wretch, and treats thee ill, there is power in the Spirit. And, O ye who have come from barren churches with scarcely a leaf upon the tree. Do not doubt the power of the Spirit to raise you up. For it shall be a "pasture for flocks, a den of wild asses," open, but deserted, until the Spirit is poured out from on high. And then the parched ground shall be made a pool, and the thirsty land springs of water, and in the habitations of dragons, where each day shall be grass with reeds and rushes. And, O ye who remember what your God has done for you especially, never distrust the power of the Spirit. Ye have seen the wilderness blossom like Carmel, ye have seen the desert blossom like the rose; trust Him for the future. Then go out and labour with this conviction, that the power of the Holy Ghost is able to do anything. Go to your Sunday-school; go to your tract distribution; go to your missionary enterprise! go to your preaching in your rooms, with the conviction that the power of the Spirit is our great help.

And now, lastly, to you sinners:—What is there to be said to you about this power of the Spirit? Why, to me, there is some hope for some of you. I cannot save you: I cannot get at you. I make you cry sometimes—you wipe your eyes, and it is all over. But I know my Master can. That is my consolation. Chief of sinners, there is hope for thee! This power can save you as well as anybody else. It is able to break your heart, though it is an iron one; to make your eyes run with tears though they have been like rocks before. His power is able this morning, if He will, to change your heart, to turn the current of all your ideas; to make you at once a child of God, to justify you in Christ. There is power enough in the Holy Spirit. Ye are not straightened in Him, but in your own bowels. He is able to bring sinners to Jesus: He is able to make you willing in the day of His power. Are you willing this morning? Has He gone so far as to make you desire His name, to make you wish for Jesus? Then, O sinner! whilst He draws you, say, "Draw me, I am wretched without thee." Follow Him, follow Him; and, while He leads, tread you in His footsteps, and rejoice that He has begun a good work in you, for there is an evidence that He will continue it even unto the end. And, O desponding one! put thy trust in the power of the Spirit. Rest on the blood of Jesus, and thy soul is safe, not only now, but throughout eternity. God bless you, my hearers. Amen.

THE HOLY GHOST—THE GREAT TEACHER

A SERMON

Text.—"Howbeit when he, the Spirit of truth, is come, he will guide you into all truth: for he shall not speak of himself; but whatsoever he shall hear, *that* shall he speak: and he will shew you things to come."—John xvi. 13.

THIS generation hath gradually, and almost imperceptibly, become to a great extent a godless generation. One of the diseases of the present generation of mankind, is their secret but deep-seated godlessness, by which they have so far departed from the knowledge of God. Science has discovered to us second causes; and hence, many have too much forgotten the first Great Cause, the Author of all: they have been able so far to pry into secrets, that the great axiom of the existence of a God, has been too much neglected. Even among professing Christians, while there is a great amount of religion, there is too little godliness: there is much external formalism, but too little inward acknowledgment of God, too little living on God, living with God, and relying upon God. Hence arises the sad fact, that when you enter many of our places of worship you will certainly hear the name of God mentioned; but except in the benediction, you would scarcely know there was a Trinity. In many places dedicated to Jehovah the name of Jesus is too often kept in the background; the Holy Spirit is almost entirely neglected; and very little is said concerning His sacred influence.

Even religious men have become to a large degree godless in this age. We sadly require more preaching regarding God; more preaching of those things which look not so much at the creature to be saved, as at God the Great One to be extolled. My firm conviction is, that in proportion as we have more regard for the sacred godhead, the wondrous Trinity in Unity, shall we see a greater display of God's power, and a more glorious manifestation of His might in our churches. May God send us a Christ-exalting, Spirit-loving ministry—men who shall proclaim God the Holy Ghost in all His offices, and shall extol God the Saviour as the author and finisher of our faith; not neglecting that Great God, the Father of His people, who before all worlds, elected us in Christ His Son, justified us through His righteousness, and will inevitably preserve us and gather us together in one, in the consummation of all things at the last great day.

Our text has regard to God the Holy Spirit; of Him we shall speak and Him only, if His sweet influence shall rest upon us.

The disciples had been instructed by Christ concerning certain elementary doctrines, but Jesus did not teach His disciples more than what we should call the A B C of religion. He gives His reasons for this in the 12th verse: "I have yet many things to say unto you, but you cannot bear them now." His disciples were not possessors of the Spirit. They had the Spirit so far as the work of conversion was concerned, but not as to the matters of bright illumination, profound instruction, prophecy, and inspiration. He says, "I am now about to depart, and when I go from you I will send the Comforter unto you. Ye cannot bear these things now, howbeit, when he, the Spirit of truth is come, he will guide you into all truth." The same promise that He made to His apostles, stands good to all His children; and in reviewing it, we shall take it as *our* portion and heritage, and shall not consider ourselves intruders upon the manor of the apostles, or upon their exclusive rights and prerogatives; for we conceive that Jesus says even to us, "When he, the Spirit of truth is come, he will guide you into all truth."

Dwelling exclusively upon our text, we have five things. First of all, here is *an attainment mentioned*—a knowledge of all truth; secondly, here is *a difficulty suggested*—which is, that we need guidance into all truth: thirdly, here is *a person provided*—"when he, the Spirit shall come, he shall guide you into all truth"; fourthly, here is *a manner hinted at*—"he shall guide you into all truth"; fifthly here is *a sign given as to the working of the Spirit*—we may know whether He works, by His "guiding us into *all* truth,"—into all of one thing; not *truths*, but *truth*.

I. Here is AN ATTAINMENT MENTIONED, which is a knowledge of all truth. We know that some conceive doctrinal knowledge to be of very little importance, and of no practical use. We do not think so. We believe the science of Christ crucified and a judgment of the teachings of Scripture to be exceedingly valuable; we think it is right, that the Christian ministry should not only be arousing but instructing; not merely awakening, but enlightening; that it should appeal not only to the passions but to the understanding. We are far from thinking doctrinal knowledge to be of secondary importance; we believe it to be one of the first things in the Christian life, to know the truth, and then to practise it. We scarcely need this morning tell you how desirable it is for us to be well taught in things of the kingdom.

First of all, *nature itself* (when it has been sanctified by grace) *gives us a strong desire to know all truth*. The natural man separateth himself and intermeddleth with all knowledge. God has put an instinct in him by which he is rendered unsatisfied if he cannot probe mystery to its bottom; he can never be content until he can unriddle secrets. What we call curiosity is something given us of God impelling us to search into the knowledge of natural things; that curiosity, sanctified by the Spirit, is also brought to bear in matters of heavenly science and celestial wisdom. "Bless the Lord," said David, "O my soul, and *all that is within me* bless his holy name!" If there is a curiosity within us, it ought to be employed and developed in a search after truth. "All that is within me," sanctified by the Spirit should be developed. And, verily, the Christian man feels an intense longing to bury his ignorance and receive wisdom. If he, when in his natural estate panted for terrestrial knowledge, how much more ardent is the wish to unravel, if possible, the sacred mysteries of God's Word! A true Christian is always intently reading and searching the Scripture that he may be able to certify himself as to its main and cardinal truths.

Not only is this attainment to be desired because nature teaches us so, but a knowledge of all truth is *very essential for our comfort.* I do believe that many persons have been distressed half their lives from the fact that they had not clear views of truth. Many poor souls, for instance, under conviction, abide three or four times as long in sorrow of mind as they would require to do if they had someone to instruct them in the great matter of justification. So there are believers who are often troubling themselves about falling away; but if they knew in their soul the great consolation that we are kept by the grace of God through faith unto salvation, they would be no more troubled about it. So have I found some distressed about the unpardonable sin; but if God instructs us in that doctrine, and shows us that no conscience that is really awakened ever can commit that sin, but that when it is committed God gives us up to a seared conscience, so that we never fear or tremble afterwards, all that distress would be alleviated. Depend on this, the more you know of God's truth— all things else being equal—the more comfortable you will be as a Christian. Nothing can give a greater light on your path than a clear understanding of divine things. It is a mingle-mangled gospel too commonly preached, which causes the downcast faces of Christians. Give me the congregation whose faces are bright with joy, let their eyes glisten at the sound of the gospel, then will I believe that it is God's own words they are receiving. Instead thereof you will often see melancholy congregations whose visages are not much different from the bitter countenance of poor creatures swallowing medicine, because the word spoken terrifies them by its legality, instead of comforting them by its grace. We love a cheerful gospel, and we think "all the truth" will tend to comfort the Christian.

Again, I hold also that this attainment to the knowledge of all truth is very desirable for *the usefulness which it will give us in the world at large.* We should not be selfish: we should always consider whether a thing will be beneficial to others. A knowledge of all truth will make us very serviceable in this world. We shall be skilful physicians who know how to take the poor distressed soul aside, to put the finger on his eye, and take the scale off for him, that heaven's light may comfort him. There will be no character, however perplexing may be its peculiar phase, but we shall be able to speak to it and comfort it. He who holds the truth, is usually the most useful man As a good Presbyterian brother said to me the other day: "I know God has blessed you exceedingly in gathering in souls, but it is an extraordinary fact that nearly all the men I know—with scarcely an exception—who have been made useful in gathering in souls, have held the great doctrines of the grace of God." Almost every man whom God has blessed to the building up of the church in prosperity, and around whom the people have rallied, has been a man who has held firmly free grace from first to last, through the finished salvation of Christ.

II. Now, again, here is a DIFFICULTY SUGGESTED, and that is— that we require a guide to conduct us into all truth. The difficulty is that truth is not so easy to discover. There is no man born in this world by nature who has the truth in his heart. There is no creature that ever was fashioned, since the fall, who has a knowledge of truth innate and natural. It has been disputed by many philosophers whether there are such things as innate ideas at all. But is of no use disputing as to whether there are any innate ideas of truth. There are none such. There are ideas of everything that is wrong and evil; but in us—that is our flesh—there dwelleth no *good* thing; we are born in sin, and shapened in iniquity; in sin did our mother conceive us. There is nothing in us good, and no tendency to righteousness. Then, since we are not born with the truth, we have the task of searching for it. If we are to be blest by being eminently useful as Christian men, we must be well instructed in matters of revelation; but here is the difficulty—that we cannot follow without a guide the winding paths of truth. Why this?

First, because of *the very great intricacy of truth itself.* Truth itself is no easy thing to discover. Those who fancy they know everything and constantly dogmatise with the spirit of "We are the men, and wisdom will die with us," of course see no difficulties whatever in the system they hold; but I believe, the most earnest student of Scripture will find things in the Bible which puzzle him; however earnestly he reads it, he will see some mysteries too deep for him to understand. He will cry out "Truth! I cannot find thee; I know not where thou art, thou art beyond me; I cannot fully view thee." Truth is a path so narrow that two can scarce walk together in it; we usually tread the narrow way in single file; two men can seldom walk arm in arm in the truth. We believe the same truth in the main but we cannot walk together in the path, it is too narrow. The way of truth is very difficult. If you step an inch aside on the right you are in a dangerous error, and if you swerve a little to the left you are equally in the mire. On the one hand there is a huge precipice, and on the other a deep morass; and unless you keep to the true line, to the breadth of a hair, you will go astray. Truth is a narrow path indeed. It is a path the eagle's eye hath not seen, and a depth the diver hath not visited. It is like the veins of metal in a mine, it is often of excessive thinness, and moreover it runneth not in one continued layer. Lose it once, and you may dig for miles and not discover it again; the eye must watch perpetually the direction of the lode. Grains of truth are like the grains of gold in the rivers of Australia —they must be shaken by the hand of patience, and washed in the stream of honesty, or the fine gold will be mingled with sand. Truth is often mingled with error, and it is hard to distinguish it; but we bless God it is said, "When the Spirit of truth is come, he will guide you into all truth."

Another reason why we need a guide is, *the invidiousness of error.* It easily steals upon us, and, if I may so describe our position, we are often like we were on Thursday night in that tremendous fog. Most of us were feeling for ourselves, and wondering where on earth we were. We could scarcely see an inch before us. We came to a place where there were three turnings. We thought we knew the old spot. There was the lamp-post, and now we must take a sharp turn to the left. But not so. We ought to have gone a little to the right. We have been so often to the same place, that we think we know every flag-stone;—and there's our friend's shop over the way. It is dark, but we think we must be quite right, and all the while we are quite wrong, and find ourselves half-a-mile out of the way. So it is with matters of truth. We think, surely this is the right path; and the voice of the evil one whispers, "that is the way, walk ye in it." You do so, and you find to your great dismay, that instead of the path of truth, you have been walking in the paths of unrighteousness and erroneous doctrines. The way of life is a labyrinth; the grassiest paths and the most bewitching, are the farthest away from right; the most enticing, are those which are garnished with wrested truths. I believe there is not a counterfeit coin in the world so much like a genuine one, as some errors are like the truth. One is base metal, the other is true gold; still in externals they differ very little.

We also need a guide, because *we are so prone to go astray.* Why, if the path of heaven were as straight as Bunyan pictures it, with no turning to the right hand or left—and no doubt it is,—we are so prone to go astray, that we should go to the right hand to the Mountains of Destruction, or to the left in the dark Wood of Desolation. David says, "I have gone astray like a lost sheep." That means very often: for if a sheep is put into a field twenty times, if it does not get out twenty-one times, it will be because it cannot; because the place is hurdled up, and it cannot find a hole in the hedge. If grace did not guide a man, he would go astray, though there were hand-posts all the way to heaven. Let it be written, "Miklat, Miklat, the way to refuge," he would turn aside, and the avenger of blood would overtake him, if some guide did not, like the angels in Sodom, put his hand on his shoulders, and cry, "Escape, escape, for thy life! look not behind thee; stay not in all the plain." These, then, are the reasons why we need a guide.

III. In the third place, here is A PERSON PROVIDED. This is none other than God, and this God is none other than a person. This person is "he, the Spirit," the "Spirit of truth"; not an influence or an emanation, but actually a person. "When the Spirit of truth is come, he shall guide you into all truth." Now, we wish you to look at this guide, to consider how adapted He is to us.

In the first place, He is *infallible;* He knows everything and cannot lead us astray. If I pin my sleeve to another man's coat, he may lead me part of the way rightly, but by-and-bye he will go wrong himself, and I shall be led astray with him. But if I give myself to the Holy Ghost and ask His guidance, there is no fear of my wandering.

Again, we rejoice in this Spirit because He is *ever-present.* We fall into a difficulty sometimes; we say, "Oh, if I could take this to my minister, he would explain it; but I live so far off, and am not able to see him." That perplexes us, and we turn the text round and round and cannot make anything out of it. We look at the commentators. We take down pious Thomas Scott, and, as usual, he says nothing about it if it be a dark passage. Then we go to holy Matthew Henry, and if it is an easy Scripture, he is sure to explain it; but if it is a text hard to be understood, it is likely enough, of course, left in his own gloom. And even Dr. Gill himself, the most consistent of commentators, when he comes to a hard passage, manifestly avoids it in some degree. But when we have no commentator or minister, we have still the Holy Spirit. And let me tell you a little secret: whenever you cannot understand a text, open your Bible, bend your knee, and pray over that text; and if it does not split into atoms and open itself, try again. If prayer does not explain it, it is one of the things God did not intend you to know, and you may be content to be ignorant of it. Prayer is the key that openeth the cabinets of mystery. Prayer and faith are sacred picklocks that can open secrets, and obtain great treasures. There is no college for holy education like that of the blessed Spirit, for He is an ever-present tutor, to Whom we have only to bend the knee, and He is at our side, the great expositor of truth.

But there is one thing about the suitability of this guide which is remarkable. I do not know whether it has struck you—the Holy Spirit can "guide us *into* a truth." Now, man can guide us *to* a truth, but it is only the Holy Spirit who can "guide us *into* a truth." "When he, the Spirit of truth, shall come, he shall guide you *into*"—mark that word—"all truth." Now, for instance, it is a long while before you can lead some people to election; but when you have made them see its correctness, you have not led them "*into*" it. You may show them that it is plainly stated in Scripture, but they will turn away and hate it. You take them to another great truth, but they have been brought up in a different fashion, and though they cannot answer your arguments, they say, "The man is right, perhaps," and they whisper—but so low that conscience itself cannot hear—"but it is so contrary to my prejudices, that I cannot receive it." After you have led them *to* the truth, and they see it is true, how hard it is to lead them *into* it! There are many of my hearers who are brought *to* the truth of their depravity; but they are not brought *into* it, and made to feel it. Some of you are brought to know the truth that God keeps us from day to day; but you rarely get into it, so as to live in continual dependence upon God the Holy Ghost, and draw fresh supplies from Him. The thing is—to get inside it. A Christian should do with truth as a snail does with his shell—live inside it, as well as carry it on his back, and bear it perpetually about with him. The Holy Ghost, it is said, shall lead us into all truth. You may be brought to a chamber where there is an abundance of gold and silver, but you will be no richer unless you effect an entrance. It is the Spirit's work to unbar the two-leaved gates, and bring us into a truth, so that we may get inside it, and, as dear old Rowland Hill said, "Not only hold the truth, but have the truth hold us."

IV. Fourthly, here is A METHOD SUGGESTED: "He shall guide you into all truth." Now I must have an illustration. I must compare truth to some cave or grotto that you have heard of, with wondrous stalactites hanging from the roof, and others starting from the floor; a cavern, glittering with spar and abounding in marvels. Before entering the cavern you inquire for a guide, who comes with his lighted flambeau. He conducts you down to a considerable depth, and you find yourself in the midst of the cave. He leads you through different chambers. Here he points to a little stream rushing from amid the rocks, and indicates its rise and progress; there he points to some peculiar rock and tells you its name; then takes you into a large natural hall, tells you how many persons once feasted in it; and so on. Truth is a grand series of caverns, it is our glory to have so great and wise a conductor. Imagine that we are coming to the darkness of it. He is a light shining in the midst of us to guide us. And by the light he shows us wondrous things. In three ways the Holy Ghost teaches us: by suggestion, direction, and illumination.

First, He guides us into all truth *by suggesting it*. There are thoughts that dwell in our minds that were not born there, but which were exotics brought from heaven and put there by the spirit. It is not a fancy that angels whisper into our ears, and that devils do the same: both good and evil spirits hold converse with men; and some of us have known it. We have had strange thoughts which were not the offspring of our souls, but which came from angelic visitants; and direct temptations and evil insinuations have we had which were not brewed in our own souls, but which came from the pestilential cauldron of hell. So the Spirit doth speak in men's ears, sometimes in the darkness of the night. In ages gone by He spoke in dreams and visions, but now He speaketh by His Word. Have you not at times had unaccountably in the middle of your business a thought concerning God and heavenly things, and could not tell whence it came? Have you not been reading or studying the Scripture, but a text came across your mind, and you could not help it; though you even put it down it was like cork in water, and would swim up again to the top of your mind. Well, that good thought was put there by the Spirit; He often guides His people into all truth by suggesting just as the guide in the grotto does with his flambeau. He does not say a word, perhaps, but he walks into a passage himself, and you follow him; so the Spirit suggests a thought, and your heart follows it up.

Well can I remember the manner in which I learned the doctrines of grace in a single instant. Born, as all of us are by nature, an Arminian, I still believed the old things I had heard continually from the pulpit, and did not see the grace of God. I remember sitting one day in the house of God and hearing a sermon as dry as possible, and as worthless as all such sermons are, when a thought struck my mind—how came I to be converted? I prayed, thought I. Then I thought how came I to pray? I was induced to pray by reading the Scriptures. How came I to read the Scriptures? Why—I did read them; and what led me to that? And then, in a moment, I saw that God was at the bottom of all, and that He was the author of faith. And then the whole doctrine opened up to me, from which I have not departed.

But sometimes He leads us *by direction*. The guide points and says—"There, gentlemen, go along that particular path; that is the way." So the Spirit gives a direction and tendency to our thoughts; not suggesting a new one but letting a particular thought when it starts take such-and-such a direction; not so much putting a boat on the stream as steering it when it is there. When our thoughts are considering sacred things He leads us into a more excellent channel from that in which we started. Time after time have you commenced a meditation on a certain doctrine and, unaccountably, you were gradually led away into another, and you saw how one doctrine leaned on another, as is the case with the stones in the arch of a bridge, all hanging on the keystone of Jesus Christ crucified. You were brought to see these things not by a new idea suggested, but by direction given to your thoughts.

But perhaps the best way in which the Holy Ghost leads us into all truth is by *illumination*. He illuminates the Bible. Now, have any of you an illuminated Bible at home? "No," says one, "I have a morocco Bible; I have a marginal reference Bible." Ah! that is all very well; but have you an illuminated Bible? "Yes; I have a large family Bible with pictures in it." There is a picture of John the Baptist baptizing Christ by pouring water on His head and many other nonsensical things; but that is not what I mean; have you an illuminated Bible? "Yes; I have a Bible with splendid engravings in it." Yes; I know you may have; but have you an illuminated Bible? "I don't understand what you mean by an illuminated Bible." Well, it is the Christian man who has an illuminated Bible. He does not buy it illuminated originally, but when he reads it

> " A glory gilds the sacred page,
>   Majestic like the sun;
>   Which gives a light to every age,—
>   It gives, but borrows none."

There is nothing like reading an illuminated Bible, beloved. You may read to all eternity, and never learn anything by it, unless it is illuminated by the Spirit; and then the words shine forth like stars. The book seems made of gold leaf; every single letter glitters like a diamond. Oh! it is a blessed thing to read an illuminated Bible lit up by the radiance of the Holy Ghost. Hast thou read the Bible and studied it, my brother, and yet have thine eyes been unenlightened? Go and say, "O Lord, gild the Bible for me. I want an expounded Bible. Illuminate it; shine upon it; for I cannot read it to profit, unless thou enlightenest me." Blind men may read the Bible with their fingers, but blind souls cannot. We want a light to read the Bible by; there is no reading it in the dark. Thus the Holy Spirit leads us into all truth, by suggesting ideas, by directing our thoughts, and by illuminating the Scriptures when we read them.

V. The last thing is AN EVIDENCE. The question arises, How may I know whether I am enlightened by the Spirit's influence, and led into all truth? First, you may know the Spirit's influence by its *unity*—He guides us into all *truth* : secondly, by its *universality*—He guides us into *all* truth.

First, if you are judging a minister, whether he has the Holy Ghost in him or not, you may know him in the first place, by *the constant unity of his testimony*. A man cannot be enlightened by the Holy Spirit, who preaches yea and nay. The Spirit never says one thing at one time and another thing at another time. There are indeed many good men who say both yea and nay; but still their contrary testimonies are not both from God the Spirit, for God the Spirit cannot witness to black and white, to a falsehood and truth. It has been always held as a first principle, that truth is one thing. But some persons say, "I find one thing in one part of the Bible and another thing in another, and though it contradicts itself I must believe it." All quite right, brother, if it did contradict itself; but the fault is not in the wood but in the carpenter. Many carpenters do not understand dove-tailing; so there are many preachers who do not understand dove-tailing. It is very nice work, and it is not easily learnt; it takes some apprenticeship to make all doctrines square together.

And you may know it by its *universality*. The true child of God will not be led into some truth but into all truth. When first he starts he will not know half the truth, he will believe it but not understand it; he will have the germ of it but not the sum total in all its breadth and length. There is nothing like learning by experience. A man cannot set up for a theologian in a week. Certain doctrines take years to develop themselves. Like the aloe that taketh a hundred years to be dressed, there be some truths that must lie long in the heart before they really come out and make themselves appear so that we can speak of them as that we do know, and testify of that which we have seen. The Spirit will gradually lead us into all truth. For instance, if it be true that Jesus Christ is to reign upon the earth personally for a thousand years, as I am inclined to believe it is, if I be under the Spirit, that will be more and more opened to me, until I with confidence declare it. Some men begin very timidly. A man says, at first, "I know we are justified by faith, and have peace with God, but so many have cried out against eternal justification, that I am afraid of it." But he is gradually enlightened, and led to see that in the same hour when all his debts were paid, a full discharge was given; that in the moment when its sin was cancelled, every elect soul was justified in God's mind, though they were not justified in their own minds till afterwards. The Spirit shall lead you into all truth.

Now, what are the practical inferences from this great doctrine? The first is with reference to the Christian who is afraid of his own ignorance. How many are there who are just enlightened and have tasted of heavenly things, who are afraid they are too ignorant to be saved! Beloved, God the Holy Spirit can teach any one, however illiterate, however uninstructed. I have known some men who were almost idiots before conversion, but they afterwards had their faculties wonderfully developed. Some time ago there was a man who was so ignorant that he could not read, and he never spoke anything like grammar in his life, unless by mistake; and moreover, he was considered to be what the people in his neighbourhood called "daft." But when he was converted, the first thing he did was to pray. He stammered out a few words, and in a little time his powers of speaking began to develop themselves. Then he thought he would like to read the Scriptures, and after long, long months of labour, he learned to read. And what was the next thing? He thought he could preach; and he did preach a little in his own homely way, in his house. Then he thought "I must read a few more books." And so his mind expanded, until, I believe he is at the present day, a useful minister, settled in a country village, labouring for God. It needs but little intellect to be taught of God. If you feel your ignorance, do not despair. Go to the Spirit—the great Teacher—and ask his sacred influence; and it shall come to pass that He "shall guide you into all truth."

Another inference is this: whenever any of our brethren do not understand the truth let us take a hint as to the best way of dealing with them. Do not let us controvert with them. I have heard many controversies, but never heard of any good from one of them. Few men are taught by controversy, for

" A man convinced against his will, is of the same opinion still."

Pray for them that the Spirit of truth may lead them "into all truth." Do not be angry with your brother, but pray for him; cry, "Lord! open thou his eyes that he may behold wondrous things out of thy law."

Lastly, we speak to some of you who know nothing about the Spirit of truth, nor about the truth itself. It may be that some of you are saying, "We care not much which of you are right, we are happily indifferent to it." Ah! but, poor sinner, if thou knewest the gift of God, and who it was that spake the truth, thou would'st not say, "I care not for it"; if thou didst know how essential the truth is to thy salvation, thou wouldst not talk so; if thou didst know that the truth of God is—that thou art a worthless sinner, but if thou believest, then God from all eternity, apart from all thy merits, loved thee, and bought thee with the Redeemer's blood, and justified thee in the forum of heaven, and will by-and-bye justify thee in the forum of thy conscience through the Holy Ghost by faith; if thou didst know that there is a heaven for thee beyond the chance of a failure, a crown for thee, the lustre of which can never be dimmed; —then thou wouldst say, "Indeed the truth is precious to my soul!" Why, my ungodly hearers, these men of error want to take away the truth, which alone can save you, the only gospel that can deliver you from hell; they deny the great truths of free-grace, those fundamental doctrines which alone can snatch a sinner from hell; and even though you do not feel interest in them now, I still would say, you ought to desire to see them promoted. May God give you to know the truth in your hearts! May the Spirit "guide you into all truth!" For if you do not know the truth here, recollect there will be a sorrowful learning of it in the dark chambers of the pit, where the only light shall be the flames of hell! May you here know the truth! And the truth shall make you free: and if the Son shall make you free, you shall be free indeed, for He says, "I am the way, the truth, the life." Believe on Jesus thou chief of sinners; trust His love and mercy, and thou art saved, for God the Spirit giveth faith and eternal life.

THE OUTPOURING OF THE HOLY SPIRIT

A SERMON

Text.—"While Peter yet spake these words, the Holy Ghost fell on all them which heard the Word."—Acts x. 44.

THE Bible is a book of the Revelation of God. The God after whom the heathen blindly searched, and for whom reason gropes in darkness, is here plainly revealed to us in the pages of divine authorship, so that he who is willing to understand as much of Godhead as man can know, may here learn it if he be not willingly ignorant and wilfully obstinate. The doctrine of the Trinity is specially taught in Holy Scripture. The word certainly does not occur, but the three divine persons of the One God are frequently and constantly mentioned, and Holy Scripture is exceedingly careful that we should all receive and believe that great truth of the Christian religion, that the Father is God, that the Son is God, that the Spirit is God, and yet there are not three Gods but one God: though they be each of them very God of very God, yet three in one and one in three is the Jehovah whom we worship.

You will notice in the works of *Creation* how carefully the Scriptures assure us that all the three divine persons took their share. "In the beginning Jehovah created the heavens and the earth"; and in another place we are told that God said "Let *us* make man"—not one person, but all three taking counsel with each other with regard to the making of mankind. We know that the Father hath laid the foundations and fixed those solid beams of light on which the blue arches of the sky are sustained; but we know with equal certainty that Jesus Christ, the eternal *Logos*, was with the Father in the beginning, and "without him was not anything made that was made": moreover we have equal certainty that the Holy Spirit had a hand in Creation, for we are told that "the earth was without form and void, and darkness was upon the face of the earth; and the spirit of the Lord moved upon the face of the waters"; and brooding with His dove-like wing, He brought out of the egg of chaos this mighty thing, the fair round world.

We have the like proof of the three persons in the Godhead in the matter of *Salvation*. We know that God the Father gave His Son; we have abundant proof that God the Father chose His people from before the foundation of the world, that He did invent the plan of salvation, and hath always given His free, willing, and joyous consent to the salvation of His people. With regard to the share that the Son had in salvation, that

is apparent enough to all. For us men and for our salvation
He came down from heaven; He was incarnate in a mortal
body; He was crucified, dead, and buried; He descended into
hades; the third day He rose again from the dead; He ascended
into heaven; He sitteth at the right hand of God, where also
He maketh intercession for us. As to the Holy Spirit, we have
equally sure proof that the Spirit of God worketh in conversion;
for everywhere we are said to be begotten of the Holy Spirit;
continually it is declared, that unless a man be born again
from above, he cannot see the kingdom of God; while all the
virtues and the graces of Christianity are described as being
the fruits of the Spirit, because the Holy Spirit doth from first
to last work in us and carry out that which Jesus Christ hath
beforehand worked for us in His great redemption, which also
God the Father hath designed for us in His great predestinating
scheme of salvation.

Now, it is to the work of the Holy Spirit that I shall this
morning specially direct your attention; and I may as well
mention the reason why I do so. It is this. In the United States
of America there has been a great awakening.* Two hundred
and fifty thousand persons—that is a quarter of a million—profess
to have been regenerated, and have united themselves with
different sections of God's church. And that which makes me
believe the work to be genuine is just this—that the enemies of
Christ's holy gospel are exceedingly wroth at it. When the
devil roars at anything, you may rest assured there is some good
in it. The devil is not like some dogs we know of; he never
barks unless there is something to bark at. When Satan howls,
we may rest assured he is afraid his kingdom is in danger. Now
this great work in America has been manifestly caused by the
outpouring of the Spirit, for no one minister has been a leader
in it. All the ministers of the gospel have co-operated in it,
but none of them have stood in the van. God Himself has been
the leader of His own hosts. It began with a desire for prayer.
God's people began to pray; the prayer-meetings were better
attended than before; it was then proposed to hold meetings
at times that had never been set apart for prayer; these also
were well attended. And there has been real prayer. Sinners
beyond all count, have risen up in the prayer-meeting, and
have requested the people of God to pray for them; thus making
public to the world that they had a desire after Christ; they
have been prayed for, and the church has seen that God verily
doth hear and answer prayer.

Now, if we have the like effect produced in this land, the one
thing we must seek is the outpouring of the Holy Spirit, and I

*The great revival of 1858, afterwards experienced in Britain.

thought, perhaps, this morning in preaching upon the work of the Holy Spirit, that text might be fulfilled—"Him that honoureth me I will honour." My sincere desire is to honour the Holy Spirit this morning, and if He will be pleased to honour His church in return, unto Him shall be the glory for ever.

"While Peter yet spake these words, the Holy Ghost fell on all them which heard the word."

In the first place, I shall endeavour to describe *the method of the Spirit's operation;* secondly, *the absolute necessity of the Holy Spirit's influence,* if we could see men converted; and then, in the third place, I shall suggest the ways and means by which under divine grace we may obtain a like falling down of the Spirit upon our churches.

1. In the first place, then, I will endeavour to explain THE METHOD OF THE HOLY SPIRIT'S OPERATIONS. But let me guard myself against being misunderstood. We can explain what the Spirit does, but how He does it, no man must pretend to know. The work of the Holy Spirit is the peculiar mystery of the Christian religion. Almost any other thing is plain, but this must remain an inscrutable secret into which it were wrong for us to attempt to pry. Who knoweth where the winds are begotten? Who knoweth, therefore, how the Spirit worketh, for He is like the wind? "The wind bloweth where it listeth, and thou hearest the sound thereof, but canst not tell whence it cometh, and whither it goeth: so is every one that is born of the Spirit." I take it that the Holy Spirit's work in conversion is two-fold. First, it is an awakening of the powers that man already has, and secondly, it is an implantation of powers which he never had at all.

In the great work of the new birth, the Holy Spirit first of all *awakens the mental powers;* for be it remembered that, the Holy Spirit never gives any man new *mental* powers. Take for instance reason—the Holy Spirit does not give men reason, for they have reason prior to their conversion. What the Holy Spirit does is to teach our reason, right reason—to set our reason in the right track, so that we can use it for the high purpose of discerning between good and evil; between the precious and vile. The Holy Spirit does not give man a will, for man has a will before; but He makes the will that was in bondage to Satan free to the service of God. The Holy Spirit gives no man the power to think, or the organ of belief—for man has power to believe or think as far as the mental act is concerned; but He gives that belief which is already there a tendency to believe the right thing, and He gives to the power of thought the propensity to think in the right way, so that instead of thinking irregularly, we begin to think as God would have us think, and our mind desireth to walk in the steps of God's revealed truth.

There may be here, this morning, a man of enlarged understanding in things political—but his understanding is darkened with regard to spiritual things—he sees no beauty in the person of Christ—he sees nothing desirable in the way of holiness—he chooses the evil and forsakes the good. Now the Holy Spirit will not give him a new understanding, but He will cleanse his old understanding so that he will discern between things that differ, and shall discover that it is but a poor thing to enjoy "the pleasures of sin for a season," and let go an "eternal weight of glory." There shall be a man here too who is desperately set against religion, and willeth not to come to God, and do what we will, we are not able to persuade him to change his mind and turn to God. The Holy Spirit will not make a new will in that man, but He will turn his old will, and instead of willing to do evil He will make him will to do right—He will make him will to be saved by Christ—He will make him "willing in the day of his power."

Remember, there is no power in man so fallen but that the Holy Spirit can raise it up. However debased a man may be, in one instant, by the miraculous power of the Spirit, all his faculties may be cleansed and purged. Ill-judging reason may be made to judge rightly; stout, obstinate will may be made to run willingly in the ways of God's commandments; evil and depraved affections may in an instant be turned to Christ, and old desires that are tainted with vice, may be replaced by heavenly aspirations. The work of the Spirit on the mind is the re-modelling of it; the new forming of it. He doth not bring new materials to the mind—it is in another part of the man that He puts up a new structure—but He puts the mind that had fallen out of order into its proper shape. He builds up pillars that had fallen down, and erects the palaces that had crumbled to the earth. This is the first work of the Holy Spirit upon the mind of man.

Besides this, the Holy Spirit gives to men *powers which they never had before*. According to Scripture, I believe man is constituted in a three-fold manner. He has a body; by the Holy Spirit that body is made the temple of the Lord. He has a mind; by the Holy Spirit that mind is made like an altar in the temple. But man by nature is nothing higher than that; he is mere body and soul. When the Spirit comes, He breathes into him a third higher principle which we call the spirit. The apostle describes man as man, "body, soul and spirit." Now if you search all the mental writers through, you will find they all declare there are only two parts—body and mind; and they are quite right, for they deal with unregenerate man; but in regenerate man there is a third principle as much superior to mere mind as mind is superior to dead animal matter—that third principle is that with which a man prays; it is that with which he savingly believes; or rather it is that which compels the mind to perform their acts. It is that which, operating upon the mind, makes the same use of the mind as the mind does of the body. When, after desiring to walk I make my legs move, it is my mind that compels them; and so my Spirit, when I desire to pray, compels my mind to think the thought of prayer and compels my soul also, if I desire to praise, to think the thought of praise, and lift itself upward towards God. As the body without the soul is dead, so the soul without the Spirit is dead, and one work of the Spirit is to quicken the dead soul by breathing into it the living Spirit; as it is written, "The first man, Adam, was made a living *soul*, but the second Adam was made a quickening *Spirit*" —and, "as we have borne the image of the earthy, so must we bear the image of the heavenly"; that is, we must have in us, if we would be converted, the quickening Spirit, which is put into us by God the Holy Ghost.

I say again, the spirit has powers which the mind never has. It has the power of communion with Christ, which to a degree is a mental act, but it can no more be performed by man without the Spirit, than the act of walking could be performed by man, if he were destitute of a soul to suggest the idea of walking. The Spirit suggests the thoughts of communion which the mind obeys and carries out. Nay, there are times, I think, when the spirit leaves the mind altogether; times when we forget everything of earth, and one almost ceases to think, to reason, to judge, to weigh, or to will. Our souls are like the chariots of Amminadib, drawn swiftly onwards without any powers of volition. We lean upon the breast of Jesus, and in rhapsody divine, and in ecstasy celestial, we enjoy the fruits of the land of the blessed, and pluck the clusters of Eschol before entering into the land of promise.

I think I have clearly put these two points before you. The work of the Spirit consists, first, in awakening powers already possessed by man, but which were asleep and out of order; and in the next place in putting into man powers which he had not before. And to make this simple to the humblest mind, let me suppose man to be something like a machine; the wheels are out of order, the cogs do not strike upon each other, the wheels do not turn regularly, the rods will not act, the order is gone. Now, the first work of the Spirit is to put these wheels in the right place, to fit the wheels upon the axles, to put the right axle to the right wheel, then to put wheel to wheel, so

D

that they may act upon each other. But that is not all His work. The next thing is to put fire and steam so that these things shall go to work. He does not put fresh wheels, He puts old wheels into order, and then He puts the motive power which is to move the whole. First He puts our mental powers into their proper order and condition, and then He puts a living quickening spirit, so that all these shall move according to the holy will and law of God.

And I must say, before I leave this point, that all the former part of what I have mentioned is done instantaneously. When a man is converted to God, it is done in a moment. Regeneration is an instantaneous work. Conversion to God, the fruit of regeneration, occupies all our life, but regeneration itself is effected in an instant. A man hates God; the Holy Spirit makes him love God. A man is opposed to Christ, he hates His gospel, does not understand it and will not receive it: the Holy Spirit comes, puts light into his darkened understanding, takes the chain from his bondaged will, gives liberty to his conscience, gives life to his dead soul, so that the voice of conscience is heard, and the man becomes a new creature in Christ Jesus. And all this is done, mark you, by the instantaneous supernatural influence of God the Holy Ghost working as He willeth among the sons of men.

II. Having thus dwelt upon the method of the Holy Spirit's work, I shall now turn to the second point, THE ABSOLUTE NECESSITY OF THE SPIRIT'S WORK IN ORDER TO CONVERSION. In our text we are told that "while Peter spake these words, the Holy Ghost fell on all them which heard the word." Beloved, the Holy Ghost fell on Peter first, or else it would not have fallen on his hearers. There is a necessity that the preacher himself, if we are to have souls saved, should be under the influence of the Spirit. I have constantly made it my prayer that I might be guided by the Spirit even in the smallest and least important parts of the service; for you cannot tell but that the salvation of a soul may depend upon the reading of a hymn, or upon the selection of a chapter. Two persons have joined our church and made a profession of being converted simply through my reading a hymn—

"Jesus, lover of my soul."

They did not remember anything else in the hymn; but those words made such a deep impression upon their mind, that they could not help repeating them for days afterwards, and then the thought arose, "Do I love Jesus?" And then they considered what strange ingratitude it was that He should be the lover of their souls, and yet they should not love Him. Now I believe the Holy Spirit led me to read that hymn. And many persons have been converted by some striking saying of the preacher. But why was it the preacher uttered that saying? Simply because he was led thereunto by the Holy Spirit.

Rest assured, beloved, that when any part of the sermon is blessed to your heart, the minister said it because he was ordered to say it by his Master. I might preach to-day a sermon which I preached on Friday, and which was useful then, and there might be no good whatever come from it now, because it might not be the sermon which the Holy Ghost would have delivered to-day. But if with sincerity of heart I have sought God's guidance in selecting the topic, and He rests upon me in the preaching of the Word, there is no fear but that it shall be found adapted to your immediate wants. The Holy Spirit must rest upon your preachers. Let them have all the learning of the wisest men, and all the eloquence of such men as Demosthenes and Cicero, still the Word cannot be blessed to you, unless first of all the Spirit of God hath guided the minister's mind in the selection of his subject, and in the discussion of it.

But if Peter himself were under the hand of the Spirit, that would fail unless the Spirit of God, then, did fall upon our hearers; and I shall endeavour now to show the absolute necessity of the Spirit's work in the conversion of men.

Let us remember what kind of thing the work is, and we shall see that other means are altogether out of the question. It is quite certain that men cannot be converted by physical means. The Church of Rome thought that she could convert men by means of armies; so she invaded countries, and threatened them with war and bloodshed unless they would repent and embrace her religion. However, it availed but little, and men were prepared to die rather than leave their faith; she therefore tried those beautiful things—stakes, racks, dungeons, axes, swords, fire; and by these things she hoped to convert men. You have heard of the man who tried to wind up his watch with a pick-axe. That man was extremely wise, compared with the man who thought to touch mind through matter. All the machines you like to invent cannot touch mind. Talk about tying angels' wings with green withes, or manacling the cherubim with iron chains, and then talk about meddling with the minds of men through physical means. Why, the things don't act; they cannot act. All the king's armies that ever were, and all the warriors clothed with mail, with all their ammunition, could never touch the mind of man. That is an impregnable castle which is not to be reached by physical agency.

Nor, again, can man be converted by moral argument. "Well," says one, "I think he may. Let a minister preach earnestly, and he may persuade men to be converted." Ah! beloved, it is for want of knowing better that you say so. Melancthon thought so, but you know what he said after he tried it—"Old Adam is too strong for young Melancthon." So will every preacher find it, if he thinks his arguments can ever convert man. Let me give you a parallel case. Where is the logic that can persuade an Ethiopian to change his skin? By what argument can you induce a leopard to renounce his spots? Even so may he that is accustomed to do evil learn to do well. But if the Ethiopian's skin be changed it must be by supernatural process; and if the leopard's spots be removed, he that made the leopard must do it. Even so is it with the heart of man. If sin were a thing *ab extra*, and external, we could induce man to change it. For instance, you may induce a man to leave off drunkenness or swearing, because those things are not a part of his nature —he has added that vice to his original depravity. But the hidden evil of the heart is beyond all moral suasion. I dare say a man might have enough argument to induce him to hang himself, but I am certain no argument will ever induce him to hang his sins, to hang his self-righteousness, and to come and humble himself at the foot of the cross; for the religion of Christ is so contrary to all the propensities of man, that it is like swimming against the stream to approach it, for the stream of man's will and man's desire is exactly the opposite of the religion of Jesus Christ.

I have seen the tears run down a man's cheeks when he has come to me in order to be united to the church of Christ, and he has said, "Sir, I wonder how it is I am here to-day; if anyone had told me a year ago that I should think as I now think, and feel as I now feel, I should have called him a born fool for his pains; I liked to spend my Sunday in pleasure, and I did not see why I was to be cooping myself up in the house of God listening to a man talk. *I* pray, sir? No, not I. I said the best providence in all the world was a good strong pair of hands, and to take care of what you got. If any man talked to me about religion, why, I would slam the door in his face, and pretty soon put him out; but the things that I loved then, I now hate, and the things that then I hated now I love, I cannot do or say enough to show how total is the change that has been wrought in me. It must have been the work of God; it could not have been wrought by me, I feel assured; it must be someone greater than myself, who could thus turn my heart." I think these two things are proofs that we want something more than nature, and since physical agency will not do, and mere moral suasion will never accomplish it, that there must be an absolute necessity for the Holy Spirit.

But again, if you will just think a minute what the work is, you will soon see that none but God can accomplish it. In the Holy Scripture, conversion is often spoken of as being a new creation. If you talk about creating yourselves, I should feel obliged if you would create a fly first. Create a gnat, create a grain of sand, and when you have created that, you may talk about creating a new heart. Both are alike, impossible, for creation is the work of God. But still, if you could create a grain of dust, or create even a world, it would not be half the miracle, for you must first find a thing which has created itself. Could that be? Suppose you had no existence, how could you create yourself? Nothing cannot produce anything. Now, how can man re-create himself? A man cannot create himself into a new condition, when he has no being in that condition, but is, as yet, a thing that is not.

Then, again, the work of creation is said to be like the resurrection. "We are alive from the dead." Now, can the dead in the grave raise themselves? Let any minister who thinks he can convert souls, go and raise a corpse; let him go and stand in one of the cemeteries, and bid the tombs open wide their mouths, and make room for those once buried there to awaken, and he will have to preach in vain. But if he could do it, that is not the miracle: it is for the dead to raise themselves, for an inanimate corpse to kindle in its own breast the spark of life anew. If the work be a resurrection, a creation, does it not strike you that it must be beyond the power of man? It must be wrought in him by no one less than God Himself.

And there is yet one more consideration, and I shall have concluded this point. Beloved, even if man could save himself, I would have you recollect how averse he is to it? If we could make our hearers all willing, the battle would be accomplished. "Well," says one, "if I am willing to be saved, can I not be saved?" Assuredly you can, but the difficulty is, we cannot bring men to be willing. That shows, therefore, that there must be a constraint put upon their will. There must be an influence exerted upon them, which they have not in themselves, in order to make them willing in the day of God's power. And this is the glory of the Christian religion. The Christian religion has within its own bowels power to spread itself. We do not ask you to be willing first. We come and tell you the news, and we believe that the Spirit of God working with us, will make you willing. If the progress of the Christian religion depended upon the voluntary assent of mankind, it would never go an inch further, but because the Christian religion has with it an omnipotent influence, constraining men to believe it, it is therefore that it is and must be triumphant, "till like a sea of glory it spreads from shore to shore."

III. Now I shall conclude by bringing one or two thoughts forward, with regard to WHAT MUST BE DONE AT THIS TIME IN ORDER TO BRING DOWN THE HOLY SPIRIT. It is quite certain, beloved, if the Holy Spirit willed to do it, that every man, woman, and child in this place might be converted now. If God, the Sovereign Judge of all, would be pleased now to send out his Spirit, every inhabitant of this million-peopled city might be brought at once to turn unto the living God. Without instrumentality, without the preacher, without books, without anything, God has it in His power to convert men. We have known persons about their business, not thinking about religion at all, who have had a thought injected into their heart, and that thought has been the prolific mother of a thousand meditations; and through these meditations they have been brought to Christ. Without the aid of the minister, the Holy Spirit has thus worked, and to-day He is not restrained. There may be some men, great in infidelity, staunch in opposition to the Cross of Christ, but, without asking their consent, the Holy Spirit can pull down the strong man, and make the mighty man bow himself. For when we talk of the Omnipotent God, there is nothing too great for Him to do.

But, beloved, God has been pleased to put great honour upon instrumentality; He could work without it if He pleased, but He does not do so. However, this is the first thought I want to give you; if you would have the Holy Spirit exert Himself in our midst, you must first of all look to Him and not to instrumentality. When Jesus Christ preached, there were very few converted under Him, and the reason was, because the Holy Spirit was not abundantly poured forth. He had the Holy Spirit without measure Himself, but on others the Holy Spirit was not as yet poured out. Jesus Christ said, "Greater works than these shall ye do because I go to my Father, in order to send the Holy Spirit"; and recollect that those few who were converted under Christ's ministry, were not converted by Him, but by the Holy Spirit that rested upon Him at that time. Jesus of Nazareth was anointed of the Holy Spirit. Now then, if Jesus Christ, the great founder of our religion, needed to be anointed of the Holy Spirit, how much more our ministers?

And now another thought. If we would have the Spirit, beloved, we must each of us try to honour Him. There are some chapels into which if you were to enter, you would never know there was a Holy Spirit. Mary Magdalen said of old, "They have taken away my Lord, and I know not where they have laid him," and the Christian might often say so, for there is nothing said about the Lord until they come to the end, and then there is just the benediction, or else you would not know that there were three persons in one God at all. Until our churches honour the Holy Spirit, we shall never see it abundantly manifested in our midst. Let the preacher always confess before he preaches that he relies upon the Holy Spirit. Let him burn his manuscript and depend upon the Holy Spirit. If the Spirit does not come to help him, let him be still and let the people go home and pray that the Spirit will help him next Sunday.

And do you also, in the use of all your agencies, always honour the Spirit? We often begin our religious meetings without prayer; it is all wrong. We must honour the Spirit; unless we put Him first, He will never make crowns for us to wear. He will get victories, but He will have the honour of them, and if we do not give to Him the honour, He will never give to us the privilege and success. And best of all, if you would have the Holy Spirit, let us meet together earnestly to pray for Him. Remember, the Holy Spirit will not come to us as a church, unless we seek Him. "For this thing will I be enquired of by the house of Israel to do it for them." "Prove me now here, saith the Lord of hosts, and see if I do not pour you out a blessing so that there shall not be room enough to receive it." Let us meet and pray, and if God doth not hear us, it will be the first time He has broken His promise. Come, let us go up to the sanctuary; let us meet together in the house of the Lord, and offer solemn supplication; and I say again, if the Lord doth not make bare His arm in the sight of all the people, it will be the reverse of all His previous actions, it will be the contrary of all His promises, and contradictory to Himself. We have only to try Him, and the result is certain. In dependence on His Spirit, if we only meet for prayer, the Lord shall bless us, and all the ends of the earth shall fear Him. O Lord, lift up Thyself because of Thine enemies; pluck Thy right hand out of Thy bosom, O Lord our God, for Christ's sake, Amen.

THE HOLY SPIRIT COMPARED TO THE WIND

A SERMON

Text.—"The wind bloweth where it listeth, and thou hearest the sound thereof, but canst not tell whence it cometh, and whither it goeth: so is every one that is born of the Spirit."—John iii. 8.

I AM not proposing to enter fully into the subject of the new birth, but to bring before you the parallel which our Saviour here draws, between the wind and the Holy Spirit. It is a remarkable fact, known I dare say to most of you, that both in the Hebrew and Greek languages the same word is used for spirit and for wind, so that our Saviour as it were rode upon the wings of the wind, while he was instructing the seeking Rabbi in the deep things of God; He caught at the very name of the wind, as a means of fastening a spiritual truth upon the memory of the enquirer, hinting to us that language should be watched by the teacher, that he may find out suitable words, and employ those which will best assist the disciple to comprehend and to retain his teaching. "The wind," said He, "bloweth," and the very same word would have been employed if He had meant to say, "The Spirit bloweth where he listeth." There was intended, doubtless, to be a very close and intimate parallel between the Spirit of God and the wind, or otherwise the great ruler of providence, who invisibly controlled the confusion of Babel, would not have fashioned human language so that the same word should stand for both. Language, as well as nature, illustrates the wisdom of God.

It is only in *His* light that we see light: may the Holy Spirit be graciously pleased to reveal Himself in His divine operations to all our waiting minds. We are taught in God's Word that the Holy Spirit comes upon the sons of men, and makes them new creatures. Until He enters them they are "dead in trespasses and sins." They cannot discern the things of God, because divine truths are spiritual and spiritually discerned, and unrenewed men are carnal, and possess not the power to search out the deep things of God. The Spirit of God new-creates the children of God, and then in their new-born spirituality, they discover and come to understand spiritual things, but not before; and, therefore, my beloved hearers, unless you *possess* the Spirit, no metaphors however simple can reveal Him to you. Let us not mention the name of the Holy Spirit without due honour. For ever blessed be Thou, most glorious Spirit, co-equal and co-eternal with the Father and with the Son; let all the angels of God worship Thee! Be Thou had in honour, world without end!

I. We will consider IN WHAT SENSE THE HOLY GHOST MAY BE COMPARED TO THE WIND.

The Spirit of God, to help the spiritually minded in their study of His character and nature condescends to compare Himself to dew, fire, oil, water, and other suggestive types; and among the rest, our Saviour uses the metaphor of wind. What was the first thought here but that of *mystery?* It was the objection on the score of mystery which our Lord was trying to remove from the mind of Nicodemus. Nicodemus in effect said, "I cannot understand it; how can it be? a man born again when he is old, created over again, and that from an invisible agency from above? How can these things be?" Jesus at once directed his attention to the wind, which is none the less real and operative because of its mysterious origin and operation. You cannot tell whence the wind cometh: you know it blows from the north or from the west, but at what particular place does that wind start on its career? Where will it pause in its onward flight? You see that it is blowing to the east or to the west, but where is its halting-place? Whence came these particles of air which rush so rapidly past? Whither are they going? By what law are they guided in their course, and where will their journey end? The gale may be blowing due east here, but it may be driving west a hundred miles away. In one district the wind may be rushing from the north, and yet not far from it there may be a strong current from the south. If you have watched the skies, you must occasionally have noticed a stream of clouds hurrying to the right, while higher up, another company is sailing to the left.

The philosopher may scheme some conjecture to prove that the "trade winds" blow at certain intervals because of the sun crossing the equator at those periods, and that there must necessarily be a current of air going towards the equator because of the rarefaction; but he cannot tell you why the weathercock on yonder church steeple turned this morning from south-west to due east. He cannot tell me why it is that the sailor finds that his sails are at one time filled with wind, and in a few minutes they fall loosely about, so that he must steer upon another tack if he would make headway. The various motions of the air remain a mystery to all but the infinite Jehovah.

My brethren, the like mystery is observed in the work of the Spirit of God. His person and work are not to be comprehended by the mind of man. He may be here to-night, but you cannot see Him: He speaks to one heart, but others cannot hear His voice. He is not recognizable by the unrefined senses of the unregenerate. The spiritual man discerns Him, feels Him, hears Him, and delights in Him, but neither wit nor learning can

lead a man into the secret. The believer is often bowed down
with the weight of the Spirit's glory, or lifted up upon the wings
of His majesty; but even he knows not how these feelings are
wrought in him. The fire of holy life is at seasons gently fanned
with the soft breath of divine comfort, or the deep sea of spiritual
existence stirred with the mighty blast of the Spirit's rebuke;
but still it is evermore a mystery how the eternal God comes
into contact with the finite mind of His creature man, filling all
heaven meanwhile, and yet dwelling in a human body as in a
temple—occupying all space, and yet operating upon the will,
the judgment, the mind of the poor insignificant creature called
man. We may enquire, but who can answer us? We may search,
but who shall lead us into the hidden things of the Most High?
He brooded over chaos and produced order, but who shall tell
us after what fashion He wrought? He overshadowed the Virgin
and prepared a body for the Son of God, but into this secret
who shall dare to pry? His is the anointing, sealing, comforting,
and sanctifying of the saints, but how worketh He all these
things? He maketh intercession for us according to the will of
God, He dwelleth in us and leadeth us into all truth, but who
among us can explain to his fellow the order of the divine working? Though veiled from human eye like the glory which shone
between the cherubim, we believe in the Holy Ghost, and therefore see Him; but if our faith needed sight to sustain it, we should
never believe at all.

Mystery is far from being all which the Saviour would teach
by this simile. Surely He meant to show us that the operations
of the Spirit are like the wind for *divinity*. Who can create a wind?
The most ambitious of human princes would scarcely attempt
to turn, much less to send forth the wind. These steeds of the
storm know no bit nor bridle, neither will they come at any
man's bidding. Let our senators do what they will, they will
scarcely have the madness to legislate for winds. Old Boreas,
as the heathens called him, is not to be bound with chains and
welded on earthly anvil, or in vulcanian forge. "The wind
bloweth where it listeth"; and it does so because God directeth
it and suffereth it not to stay for man, nor to tarry for the sons
of men. So with the Spirit of God. All the true operations of
the Spirit are due in no sense whatever to man, but always to
God and to His sovereign will. Revivalists may get up excitement with the best intentions, and may warm peoples' hearts
till they begin to cry out, but all this ends in nothing unless it
is divine work. Have I not said scores of times in this pulpit,
"All that is of nature's spinning, must be unravelled?" Every
particle which nature puts upon the foundation will turn out
to be but "wood, hay, and stubble," and will be consumed.

It is only "the gold, the silver, and the precious stones" of God's building that will stand the fiery test. "Ye must be born again from above," for human regenerations are a lie. Thou mayest blow with thy mouth and produce some trifling effects upon trifles as light as air; man in his zeal may set the windmills of silly minds in motion; but, truly, to stir men's hearts with substantial and eternal verities, needs a celestial breeze, such as the Lord alone can send.

Did not our Lord also intend to hint at the *sovereignty* of the Spirit's work? For what other reason did He say, "The wind bloweth where it listeth?" There is an arbitrariness about the wind, it does just as it pleases, and the laws which regulate its changes are to man unknown. "Free as the wind," we say— "the wild winds." So is the mighty working of God. It is a very solemn thought, and one which should tend to make us humble before the Lord—that we are, as to the matter of salvation, entirely in His hand! If I have a moth in my hand to-night, I can bruise its wings, or I can crush it at my will, and by no attempts of its own can it escape from me. And every sinner is absolutely in the hand of God, and, let him recollect, he is in the hand of an angry God, too. The only comfort is, that he is in the hand of a God Who for Jesus' sake, delights to have mercy upon even the vilest of the vile.

Sinner, God can give thee the Holy Spirit if He wills; but if He should say, "Let him alone," thy fate is sealed; thy damnation is sure. Dost thou tremble at this? Dost thou cry, "O God! have pity upon me?" He will hear thy cry, sinner, for there never yet was a sincere cry that went up to heaven, though it were never so feeble, but what it had an answer of peace. When one of the old saints lay dying, he could only say, "O Lord, I trust thee *languida fide,*" with a languid faith. It is poor work that, but, oh! it is safe work. You can only trust Christ with a feeble faith; if it is such a poor trembling faith that it does not grip Him, but only touches the hem of His garment, it nevertheless saves you. If you can look at Him, though it be only a great way off, yet it saves you. And, oh what a comfort this is, that you are still on pleading terms with Him and in a place of hope. "Whosoever believeth is not condemned." But, oh, do not trifle with the day of grace, lest having frequently heard the warning, and hardened thy neck just as often, thou shouldest "suddenly be destroyed, and that without remedy"; for if He shut out, none can bid thee come in; if He do but put to the iron bar, thou art shut out in the darkness of obstinacy, obduracy, and despair for ever, the victim of thine own delusions. Sinner, if God save thee; He shall have all the glory, for He hath a right to do as He will, for He says, "I will have mercy on whom I will have mercy, and I will have compassion on whom I will have compassion."

But still I think I have not yet brought out what is in the text. Do you not think that the text was intended to show the *varied methods* in which the Spirit of God works in the conversion and regeneration of men? "The wind bloweth where it listeth." Now, observe the different *force* of the wind. This afternoon the wind seemed as if it would tear up every tree, and doubtless, had they been in leaf, many of those noble princes of the forest must have stretched themselves prone upon the earth; but God takes care that in these times of boisterous gales there should be no leaf, and therefore the wind gets but little purchase with which to drag up a tree. But the wind does not always blow as it did this afternoon. On a summer's evening there is such a gentle zephyr that even the gnats who have been arranging a dance among themselves are not disturbed, but keep to their proper places. Yea, the aspen seems as if it could be quiet, though you know it keeps for ever quivering, according to the old legend, that it was the tree on which the Saviour hung, and therefore trembles still as though through fear of the sin which came upon it. 'Tis but a legend. There are times when all is still and calm, when everything is quiet, and you can scarcely detect the wind at all.

Now, just so it is with the Spirit of God. To some of us He came like a "rushing mighty wind." Oh, what tearings of soul there were then! My spirit was like a sea tossed up into tremendous waves; made, as Job says, "To boil like a pot," till one would think the deep were hoary. Oh, how that wind came crashing through my soul, and every hope I had was bowed as the trees of the wood in the tempest. Read the story of John Bunyan's conversion: it was just the same. Turn to Martin Luther: you find his conversion of the same sort. So might I mention hundreds of biographies in which the Spirit of God came like a tornado sweeping everything before it, and the men could but feel that God was in the whirlwind.

To others He comes so gently, they cannot tell when first the Spirit of God came. They recollect that night when mother prayed so with brothers and sisters, and when they could not sleep for hours, because the big tears stood in their eyes on account of sin. They recollect the Sunday-school and the teacher there. They remember that earnest minister. They cannot say exactly when they gave their hearts to God, and they cannot tell about any violent convictions. They are often comforted by that text, "One thing I know, whereas I was blind, now I see"; but they cannot get any farther: they sometimes wish they could. Well, they need not wish it, for the Spirit of God, as a sovereign, will always choose His own way of operation; and if it be but the wind of the Holy Spirit, recollect it is as saving in its gentleness as in its terror, and is as efficient to make us new creatures when it comes with the zephyr's breath as when it comes with the hurricane's force. Do not quarrel with God's way of saving you. If you are brought to the Cross be thankful for it, Christ will not mind how you got there. If you can say "He is all my salvation, and all my desire," you never came to that without the Spirit of God bringing you to it. Do not therefore think you came the wrong way, for that is impossible.

Again, the wind not only differs in force, but it differs in *direction*. We have been saying several times the wind is always shifting. Perhaps there never were two winds that did blow exactly in the same direction. I mean that if we had power to detect the minute points of the compass, there would be found some deviation in every current, although, of course, for all practical purposes, it blows from certain distinct points which the mariner marks out. Now, the Spirit of God comes from different directions. You know very well, dear friends, that sometimes the Spirit of God will blow with mighty force from one denomination of Christians; then on a sudden they seem to be left, and another body of Christians God will raise up, fill with Himself, and qualify for usefulness. In the days of Wesley and Whitefield, there was very little of the divine Spirit anywhere, except among the Methodists. I am sure they have not a monopoly of Him now. The divine Spirit blows also from other quarters. Sometimes He uses one man, sometimes another. We hear of a revival in the North of Ireland, by-and-by it is in the South of Scotland. It comes just as God wills, for direction; and you know, too, dear friends, it comes through different instrumentalities in the same Church. Sometimes the wind blows from this pulpit: God blesses me to your conversion. Another time it is from my good sister, Mrs. Bartlett's class; on a third occasion it is the Sunday-school; again, it may be another class, or the preaching of the young men, or from the individual exertion of private believers. God causes that wind to blow just which way He wills.

He works also through different texts of Scripture. *You* were converted and blessed under one text: it was quite another that was made useful to *me*. Some of you were brought to Christ by terrors, others of you by love, by sweet wooing words. The wind blows as God directs. Now, dear friends, whenever you take up a religious biography, do not sit down and say, "Now I will see whether I am just like this person." Nonsense! God never repeats Himself. Men make steel pens—thousands of grosses of them—all alike, but I will be bound to say that in quills from the common, there are no two of them precisely the same. If you look, you will soon discover that they differ in a variety of ways.

Certain gardeners cut their trees into the shape of cheeses and a number of other unnatural forms, but God's trees do not grow that way, they grow just anyhow—gnarl their roots and twist their branches. Great painters do not continually paint the same picture again, and again, and again, and my Divine Master never puts His pencil on the canvas to produce the same picture twice. Every Christian is a distinct work of grace on God's part, which has in it some originality, some portion distinct from all others. I do not believe in trying to make all history uniform. It is said that Richard III. had a hump-back. Whether he really was deformed, or whether history gave him the hump-back, I cannot tell, but it is said, that all his courtiers thought it the most beautiful hump-back that ever was seen, and they all began to grow hump-backs too; and I have known ministers who had some peculiar idiosyncrasy of experience which was nothing better than a spiritual hump-back; but their people all began to have hump-backs too—to think and talk all in the same way, and to have the same doubts and fears. Now that will not do. It is not the way in which the Most High acts with regard to the wind, and if he chooses to take all the points of the compass, and make use of them all, let us bless and glorify His Name.

Are not the different winds *various in their qualities?* Few of us like an east wind. Most of us are very glad when the wind blows from the south. Vegetation seems to love much the south-west. A stiff north-easter is enough to make us perish; and long continuance of the north, may well freeze the whole earth; while from the west, the wind seems to come laden with health from the deep blue sea; and though sometimes too strong for the sick, yet it is never a bad time when the west wind blows. The ancients all had their different opinions about wind; some were dry, some were rainy, some affected this disease, some touched this part of men, some the other. Certain it is that God's Holy Spirit has different qualities. In the Canticles He blows softly with the sweet breath of love: turn on farther, and you get that same Spirit blowing fiercely with threatening and denunciation; sometimes you find Him convincing the world "of sin, of righteousness, of judgment," that is the north wind; at other times opening up Christ to the sinner, and giving him joy and comfort; that is the south wind, that blows softly, and gives a balminess in which poor troubled hearts rejoice; and yet "all these worketh the self-same Spirit."

Indeed, my subject is all but endless, and therefore I must stay.

But even in the matter of *duration* you know how the wind will sometimes blow six weeks in this direction, and, again, continue in another direction. And the Spirit of God does not always work with us: He does as He pleases; He comes, and He goes. We may be in a happy hallowed frame at one time, and at another we may have to cry, "Come from the four winds, O breath!"

II. We will consider, in the second place, THE PARALLEL BETWEEN THE HOLY SPIRIT AND THE EFFECTS OF THE WIND.

"Thou hearest the sound thereof." Ah, that we do! The wind sometimes wails as if you could hear the cry of mariners far out at sea, or the moanings of the widows that must weep for them. And, oh! the Spirit of God sets men wailing with an exceeding bitter cry for sin, as one that is in sorrow for his first-born, "Thou hearest the sound thereof." Oh, it is a blessed sound, that wailing! Angels rejoice over "one sinner that repenteth." Then comes the wind at another time with a triumphant sound, and if there be an Æolian harp in the window, how it swells, sweeps, descends, then rises again, gives all the tones of music, and makes glad the air with its jubilant notes. So with the Holy Spirit; sometimes He gives us faith, makes us bold, full of assurance, confidence, joy and peace in believing. "Thou hearest the sound" of a full diapason of the Holy Spirit's mighty melody within the soul of man, filling him with peace and joy, and rest, and love. Sometimes the wind comes, too, with another sound as though it were contending. You heard it, perhaps, this afternoon. We who are a little in the country hear it more than you do: it is as though giants were struggling in the sky together. It seems as if two seas of air, both lashed to fury, met, and dashed against some unseen cliffs with terrible uproar. The Spirit of God comes into the soul sometimes, and makes great contention with the flesh. Oh, what a stern striving there is against unbelief, against lust, against pride, against every evil thing.

"Thou hearest the sound thereof." Thou that knowest what divine experience means, thou knowest when to go forth to fight thy sins. When thou canst hear "the sound of a going in the tops of the mulberry trees," then thou dost bestir thyself to smite thy sins. Sometimes the wind comes with a sweep as though it were going on for ever. It came past, and dashed through the trees, sweeping away the rotten branches, then away across the Alps, dashing down an avalanche in its course, still onward; and as it flew, it bore away everything that was frail and weak, and on, on, on it sped its way to some unknown goal. And thus it is sometimes the Spirit of God will come right through us, as if He were bearing us away to that spiritual

heritage which is our sure future destiny—bearing away cold-
ness, barrenness, everything before it. We do not lament then
that we do not pray, we do not believe that we cannot pray;
but "I can do everything," is our joyful shout as we are carried
on the wings of the wind. "Thou hearest the sound thereof."
I hope you have heard it sometimes in all its powerful, over-
whelming, mighty influence, till your soul has been blown
away. "Thou hearest the sound thereof."

But then the wind does something more than make a sound;
and so does the Holy Spirit. It WORKS and produces manifest
results. Just think what the wind is doing to-night. I cannot
tell at what pitch it may be now. It is just possible that in some
part of the ocean a vessel scuds along almost under bare poles;
the mariners do their best to reef the sails: away she goes: now
the mast has gone: they do their best to bear up, but they find
that in the teeth of the gale they cannot stand; the ship dashes
on the rocks, and she is wrecked.

And, oh! the Spirit of God is *a great wrecker* of false hopes
and carnal confidences. I have seen the Spirit of God come to
a sinner like a storm to a ship at sea. He had to take down the
top-gallants of his pride, and then every thread of carnal confidence had to be reefed, and then his hope itself had to be cut
away; and on, on the vessel went, until she struck a rock, and
down she went. The man from that time never dared trust in
his merits, for he had seen his merits wrecked and broken in
pieces by the wind.

The wind, too, recollect, is *a great leveller*. It always aims
at everything that is high. If you are down low in the street,
you escape its fury; but climb to the top of the Monument, or
St. Paul's, and try whether you do not feel it. Get into the
valley, it is all right. The lower branches of the trees are scarcely
moved, but the top branches are rocked to and fro by it. It
is a great leveller; so is the Holy Spirit. He never sees a man
high but He brings him down. He makes every high thought
bow before the majesty of His might; and if you have any high
thought to-night, rest assured that when the Spirit of God comes,
He will lay it low, even with the ground.

Now, do not let this make you fear the Holy Spirit. It is a
blessed thing to be rocked so as to have our hopes tested, and
it is a precious thing to have our carnal confidences shaken.
And how blessedly the wind *purifies* the atmosphere! In the
Swiss valleys there is a heaviness in the air which makes the
inhabitants unhealthy. They take quinine, and you see them
going about with big swellings in their necks. From Martigny
to Bretagne, there is a great valley in which you will see hundreds
of persons diseased. The reason is, that the air does not cir-

culate. They are breathing the same air, or some of it, that their fathers breathed before them. There seems to be no ventilation between the two parts of the giant Alps, and the air never circulates; but if they have a great storm which sweeps through the valleys, it is a great blessing to the people. And so the Spirit of God comes and cleanses out our evil thoughts and vain imaginations, and though we do not like the hurricane, yet it brings spiritual health to our soul.

Again the wind is a great *trier of the nature of things.* Here comes a great rushing up the street, it sweeps over the heaps of rubbish lying in the road, away goes all the light chaff, paper, and other things which have no weight in them; they cannot stand the brunt of its whirling power; but see, the pieces of iron, the stones, and all weighty things are left unmoved. In the country the farmer severed the chaff from the wheat by throwing it up into a current of air, and the light husks all blew away, while the heavy wheat sank on the heap, cleansed and purified.

So is the Holy Ghost the great testing power, and the result of His operations will be to show men what they are. Here is a hypocrite, he has passed muster hitherto, and reckons himself to be a true and genuine man, but there comes a blast from heaven's mighty spirit, and he finds himself to be lighter than vanity: he has no weight in him, he is driven on and has no rest, can find no peace, he hurries from one refuge of lies to another. "There is no peace, saith my God, to the wicked." Thus also we try the doctrines of men, we bring the breath of inspiration to bear upon them: do they abide the test, or are they driven away? Can you hold that truth in the presence of God? Can you cling to it and find it stable in the hour of trial? Is it a nice pleasant speculation for a sunny day when all is calm and bright, or will it bear the rough rude blast of adversity, when God's Holy Spirit is purifying you with His healthful influence? True Christians and sound doctrines have ballast and weight in them, they are not moved nor driven away, but empty professors and hollow dogmas are scattered like chaff before the wind when the Lord shall blow upon them with the breath of His Spirit. Examine yourselves therefore, try the doctrines and see if they be of God. "What is the chaff to the wheat? saith the Lord." Have root in yourselves, then will you not wither in the hot blast, nor be driven away in the tempestuous day.

Is not the Spirit moreover like unto the wind in its *developing of character*? Men get all covered with dust in the hot dusty roadside of life till they are nearly the colour of the earth itself; but they come to the hill-top of Calvary, and here they stand till

E

the wind of heaven has cleansed them from all the dust that has gathered around their garments. Oh, there is nothing like communion with the Spirit of God to counteract the earthly tendencies of a business life. There are some men that get covered with a yellow dust, till they are almost hidden by it; they can talk of nothing else but money. Gold, gold, gold, is getting to occupy nearly every thought now. I have no quarrel with money in its right place, but I do not like to see men live in it. I always try to drive away that mean and grovelling spirit which lives for nothing else but to accumulate money, but I cannot always succeed. Now the Spirit of God will make a man see his folly and put his money into its right position, and place the graces of the Christian character where men can see them and glorify God in them. Never let your business character or professional skill dim and hide your Christianity. If you do, God's Spirit will come to brighten you up, and He will have no mercy on these, but will, in love to your soul, cleanse and give lustre to God's work which is wrought in you.

I see also here a thought as to the co-operation of man and the Spirit in all Christian work. It has pleased God to make us co-workers with Him, fellow labourers, both in the matter of our own salvation, and also in the effort to benefit others. Look for a moment at yon stately bark, she moves not because of her sails, but she would not reach the desired haven without them. It is the wind which propels her forward; but the wind would not act upon her as it does, unless she had the rigging all fixed, her masts standing, and her sails all bent, so as to catch the passing breeze. But now that human seamanship has done its best, see how she flies! She will soon reach her haven with such a favouring gale as that. You have only to stand still and see how the wind bears her on like a thing of life.

And so it is with the human heart. When the Spirit comes to the soul that is ready to receive such influences, then He helps you on to Christian grace and Christian work, and makes you bear up through all opposition, till you come to the port of peace, and can anchor safely there. Without Him we can do nothing: without us He will not work. We are to preach the gospel to every creature, and while one plants, and another waters, God adds the increase. We are to work out our own salvation, but He worketh in us to will and to do of His own good pleasure. We must go up to possess the goodly land with our own spear and sword; but the hornet goes before us to drive out the foe. Jericho shall be captured by a divine and miraculous interference, but even there rams' horns shall find a work to do, and must be employed. The host of Midian shall be slain, but our cry is, "The sword of the Lord and of Gideon." We give

God all the glory, nevertheless we use the means. The water of Jordan must be sought out, and used by all who desire a cleansing like Naaman the Syrian. A lump of figs must be used if other Hezekiahs are to be healed; but the Spirit is, after all, the great Cleanser and Healer of His people Israel. The lesson is clear to all: the wind turns mills that men make; fills sails that human hands have spread; and the Spirit blesses human effort, crowns with success our labours, establishes the work of our hands upon us, and teaches us all through, that "the hand of the diligent maketh rich"; but "if a man will not work, neither shall he eat."

Another thought suggests itself to my mind in connection with the wind and human effort; it is this: How completely dependent men are upon the wind as to what it shall do for them. They are entirely at its mercy as to its time of blowing, its strength, and the direction it will take. I have already dwelt upon this thought of the sovereignty of the wind, but it comes up here in a more practical form. The steamer now can steer almost anywhere it please, and at all times it will proceed on its voyage; but the sailing-ship must tack according to the wind, and when becalmed must wait for the breeze to spring up. The sailor who is depending on the wind, anxiously looks up to the masthead to see how the breeze is shifting and turning round the vane; and he scans the heavens to see what weather he is likely to have. He would not need to care nearly so much as he does now that he is absolutely dependent on the wind if he had steam-power, so as to sail in the very teeth of the storm if he so willed. God, then, keeps us looking up to heaven by making us to be completely at His mercy as to the times and ways of giving us His helping-power. It is a blessed thing to wait on God, watching for His hand and in quiet contentment leaving all to Him. Brethren, let us do our part faithfully, spread every sail, make all as perfect as human skill and wisdom can direct, and then in patient continuance in well-doing, wait the Spirit's propitious gales, neither murmuring because He tarries, nor be taken unawares when He comes upon us in His sovereign pleasure to do that which seemeth good in His sight.

And now, my dear hearer, whether you listen often to my voice, or have now stepped in for the first time, I would like to ring this in your ear, Dost thou know the Spirit of God? If ye have not the Spirit, ye are none of His. "Ye must be born again." "What, Lord—'*must*?' Dost Thou not mean 'may?'" No, ye *must*. "Does it not mean, 'Ye can be?'" No, ye *must*. When a man says, "must," it all depends upon who he is. When God says "must," there it stands, and it cannot be questioned. There are the flames of hell: would you escape from them?

You must be born again. There are heaven's glories sparkling in their own light, would you enjoy them?—you must be born again. There is the peace and joy of a believer; would you have it?—you must be born again. What, not a crumb from off the table without this? No, not one. Not a drop of water to cool your burning tongues except you are born again. This is the one condition that never moves. God never alters it, and never will. You must, *must*, MUST. Which shall it be? Shall your will stand, or God's will? O, let God's "must" ride right over you, and bow yourselves down, and say, "Lord, I must, then I will; ah! and it has come to this—I must to-night.

'Give me Christ, or else I die.'

I have hold of the knocker of the door of Thy mercy, and I *must*, I WILL get that door open. I will never let Thee go except Thou bless me. Thou sayest *must*, Lord, and I say *must* too."

"Ye must, ye must be born again." God fulfil the "must" in each of your cases, for Jesus Christ's sake. Amen.

THE WITHERING WORK OF THE SPIRIT

A SERMON

Text.—"The voice said, Cry. And he said What shall I cry? All flesh is grass, and all the goodliness thereof is as the flower of the field: the grass withereth, the flower fadeth: because the Spirit of the Lord bloweth upon it: surely the people is grass. The grass withereth, the flower fadeth: but the word of our God shall stand for ever."—Isaiah xl. 6–8.

"Being born again, not of corruptible seed, but of incorruptible, by the word of God, which liveth and abideth for ever. For all flesh is as grass, and all the glory of man as the flower of grass. The grass withereth, and the flower thereof falleth away: but the word of the Lord endureth for ever. And this is the word which by the gospel is preached unto you."—1 Peter i. 23–25.

THE passage in Isaiah which I have just read in your hearing may be used as a very eloquent description of our mortality, and if a sermon should be preached from it upon the frailty of human nature, the brevity of life, and the certainty of death, no one could dispute the appropriateness of the text. Yet I venture to question whether such a discourse would strike the central teaching of the prophet. Something more than the decay of our material flesh is intended here; the carnal mind, the flesh in another sense, was intended by the Holy Ghost when He bade His messenger proclaim those words. It does not seem to me that a mere expression of the mortality of our race was needed in this place by the context; it would hardly keep pace with the sublime revelations which surround it, and would in some measure be a digression from the subject in hand. The notion that we are here simply and alone reminded of our mortality does not square with the New Testament exposition of it in Peter, which I have also placed before you as a text. There is another and more spiritual meaning here beside and beyond that which would be contained in the great and very obvious truth, that all of us must die.

Look at the chapter in Isaiah with care. What is the subject of it? It is the divine consolation of Zion. Zion had been tossed to and fro with conflicts; she had been smarting under the result of sin. The Lord, to remove her sorrow, bids His prophets announce the coming of the long-expected Deliverer, the end and accomplishment of all her warfare and the pardon of her iniquity. There is no doubt that this is the theme of the prophecy; and further, there is no sort of question about the next point, that the prophet goes on to foretell the coming of John the Baptist as the harbinger of the Messiah. We have no difficulty in the explanation of the passage, "Prepare ye the way of the Lord, make straight in the desert a highway for our God"; for the New Testament again and again refers this to the Baptist and his ministry. The object of the coming of the Baptist and the mission of the Messiah, whom he heralded, was the manifestation of divine glory.

Observe the fifth verse: "The glory of the Lord shall be revealed, and all flesh shall see it together: for the mouth of the Lord hath spoken it." Well, what next? Was it needful to mention man's mortality in this connection? We think not. But there is much more appropriateness in the succeeding verses, if we see their deeper meaning. Do they not mean this? In order to make room for the display of the divine glory in Christ Jesus and His salvation, there would come a withering of all the glory wherein man boasts himself; the flesh should be seen in its true nature as corrupt and dying, and the grace of God alone should be exalted. This would be seen under the ministry of John the Baptist first, and should be the preparatory work of the Holy Ghost in men's hearts, in all time, in order that the glory of the Lord should be revealed and human pride be for ever confounded.

The Spirit blows upon the flesh, and that which seemed vigorous becomes weak, that which was fair to look upon is smitten with decay; the true nature of the flesh is thus discovered, its deceit is laid bare, its power is destroyed, and there is space for the dispensation of the ever-abiding word, and for the rule of the Great Shepherd, whose words are spirit and life. There is a withering wrought by the Spirit which is the preparation for the sowing and implanting by which salvation is wrought.

The withering before the sowing was very marvellously fulfilled in the preaching of John the Baptist. Most appropriately he carried on his ministry in the desert, for a spiritual desert was all around him; he was the voice of one crying in the wilderness. It was not his work to plant, but to hew down. The fleshly religion of the Jews was then in its prime. Phariseeism stalked through the streets in all its pomp; men complacently rested in outward ceremonies only, and spiritual religion was at the lowest conceivable ebb. Here and there might be found a Simeon and an Anna, but for the most part men knew nothing of spiritual religion, but said in their hearts: "We have Abraham to our father," and this is enough. What a stir he made when he called the lordly Pharisees a generation of vipers! How he shook the nation with the declaration, "Now also the axe is laid unto the root of the trees!" Stern as Elias, his work was to level the mountains, and lay low every lofty imagination.

That word, "Repent," was as a scorching wind to the verdure of self-righteousness, a killing blast for the confidence of ceremonialism. His food and his dress called for fasting and mourning. The outward token of his ministry declared the death amid which he preached, as he buried in the waters of Jordan those who came to him. "Ye must die and be buried, even as He who is to come will save by death and burial." This was the meaning of the emblem which he set before the crowd. His typical act was as thorough in its teaching as were his words; and as if that were not enough, he warned them of a yet more searching and trying baptism with the Holy Ghost and with fire, and of the coming of One whose fan was in His hand, thoroughly to purge His floor. The Spirit in John blew as the rough north wind, searching and withering, and made him to be a destroyer of the vain gloryings of a fleshly religion, that the spiritual faith might be established.

When our Lord Himself actually appeared, He came into a withered land, whose glories had all departed. Old Jesse's stem was bare, and our Lord was the branch which grew out of his root. The sceptre had departed from Judah, and the lawgiver from between his feet, when Shiloh came. An alien sat on David's throne, and the Roman called the covenant-land his own. The lamp of prophecy burned but dimly, even if it had not utterly gone out. No Isaiah had arisen of late to console them, nor even a Jeremiah to lament their apostacy. The whole economy of Judaism was as a worn-out vesture; it had waxed old, and was ready to vanish away. The priesthood was disarranged. Luke tells us that Annas and Caiaphas were high priests that year—two in a year or at once, a strange setting aside of the laws of Moses. All the dispensation which gathered around the visible, or as Paul calls it, the "worldly" sanctuary, was coming to a close; and when our Lord had finished His work, the veil of the temple was rent in twain, the sacrifices were abolished, the priesthood of Aaron was set aside, and carnal ordinances were abrogated, for the Spirit revealed spiritual things. When He came who was made a priest, "not after the law of a carnal commandment, but after the power of an endless life," there was "a disannulling of the commandment going before for the weakness and unprofitableness thereof."

Such are the facts of history; but I am not about to dilate upon them; I am coming to your own personal histories—to the experience of every child of God. In every one of us it must be fulfilled that all that is of the flesh in us, seeing it is but as grass, must be withered, and the comeliness thereof must be destroyed. The Spirit of God, like the wind, must pass over the field of our souls, and cause our beauty to be as a fading flower. He must so convince us of sin, and so reveal ourselves to ourselves, that we shall see that the flesh profiteth nothing; that our fallen nature is corruption itself, and that "they who are in the flesh cannot please God." There must be brought home to us the sentence of death upon our former legal and carnal life, that the incorruptible seed of the Word of God, implanted by the Holy Ghost, may be in us, and abide in us for ever.

The subject of this morning is the withering work of the Spirit upon the souls of men, and when we have spoken upon it, we shall conclude with a few words upon the implanting work, which always follows where this withering work has been performed.

I. Turning then to THE WORK OF THE SPIRIT IN CAUSING THE GODLINESS OF THE FLESH TO FADE, let us first, observe that the work of the Holy Spirit upon the soul of man in withering up that which is of the flesh, is *very unexpected*. You will observe in our text, that even the speaker himself, though doubtless one taught of God, when he was bidden to cry, said, "What shall I cry?" Even he did not know that in order to the comforting of God's people, there must first be experienced a preliminary visitation. Many preachers of God's gospel have forgotten that the law is the schoolmaster to bring men to Christ. They have sown on the unbroken fallow ground, and forgotten that the plough must break the clods. We have seen too much of trying to sew without the sharp needle of the Spirit's convincing power. Preachers have laboured to make Christ precious to those who think themselves rich and increased in goods; and it has been labour in vain. It is our duty to preach Jesus Christ even to self-righteous sinners, but it is certain that Jesus Christ will never be accepted by them while they hold themselves in high esteem. Only the sick will welcome the physician. It is the work of the Spirit of God to convince men of sin, and until they are convinced of sin, they will never be led to seek the righteousness which is of God by Jesus Christ.

I am persuaded, that wherever there is a real work of grace in any soul, it begins with a pulling down: the Holy Ghost does not build on the old foundation. Wood, hay, and stubble will not do for Him to build upon. He will come as the fire, and cause a conflagration of all proud nature's Babels. He will break our bow and cut our spear in sunder, and burn our chariot in the fire. When every sandy foundation is gone, then, but not till then, behold He will lay in our souls the great foundation-stone, chosen of God, and precious.

Dost thou not see that it is divinely wise that before thou art clothed thou shouldst be stripped! What, wouldst thou have

Christ's lustrous righteousness outside whiter than any fuller can make it, and thine own filthy rags concealed within? Nay, man; they must be put away; not a single thread of thine own must be left upon thee. It cannot be that God should cleanse thee until He has made thee see somewhat of thy defilement; for thou wouldst never value the precious blood which cleanses us from all sin if thou hadst not first of all been made to mourn that thou art altogether an unclean thing.

The convincing work of the Spirit, wherever it comes, is un-expected, and even to the child of God in whom this process has still to go on, it is often startling. We begin again to build that which the Spirit of God had destroyed. Having begun in the spirit, we act as if we would be made perfect in the flesh; and then when our mistaken up-building has to be levelled with the earth, we are almost as astonished as we were when first the scales fell from our eyes. In some such condition as this was Newton when he wrote:—

> " I asked the Lord that I might grow
>   In faith and love and every grace,
> Might more of his salvation know,
>   And seek more earnestly his face.
>
> 'Twas he who taught me thus to pray,
>   And he, I trust, has answered prayer;
> But it has been in such a way
>   As almost drove me to despair.
>
> I hop'd that in some favour'd hour,
>   At once he'd answer my request,
> And by his love's constraining power.
>   Subdue my sins, and give me rest.
>
> Instead of this, he made me feel
>   The hidden evils of my heart;
> And let the angry powers of hell
>   Assault my soul in ev'ry part."

Ah, marvel not, for thus the Lord is wont to answer His people. The voice which saith, "Comfort ye, comfort ye my people," achieves its purpose by first making them hear the cry, "All flesh is grass, and all the goodliness thereof is as the flower of the field."

2. Furthermore, *this withering is after the usual order of the divine operation.* If we consider well the way of God, we shall not be astonished that He beginneth with His people by terrible things in righteousness. Observe the method of creation. I will not

venture upon any dogmatic theory of geology, but there seems to be every probability that this world has been fitted up and destroyed, refitted and then destroyed again, many times before the last arranging of it for the habitation of men. "In the beginning God created the heaven and the earth"; then came a long interval, and at length, at the appointed time, during seven days, the Lord prepared the earth for the human race. Consider then the state of matters when the great architect began His work. What was there in the beginning? Originally, nothing. When He commanded the ordering of the earth how was it? "The earth was without form and void; and darkness was upon the face of the deep." There was no trace of another's plan to interfere with the Great Architect. "With whom took he counsel, and who instructed him, and taught him in the path of judgment, and taught him knowledge, and showed to him the way of understanding." He received no contribution of column or pillar towards the temple which He intended to build. The earth was, as the Hebrew puts it, Tohu and Bohu, disorder and confusion—in a word, chaos. So it is in the new creation. When the Lord new creates us, He borrows nothing from the old man, but makes all things new. He does not repair and add a new wing to the old house of our depraved nature, but He builds a new temple for His own praise. We are spiritually without form and empty, and darkness is upon the face of our heart, and His word comes to us, saying, "Light be," and there is light, and ere long life and every precious thing.

To take another instance from the ways of God. When man has fallen, when did the Lord bring him to the gospel? The first whisper of the gospel, as you know, was, "I will put enmity between thee and the woman, between thy seed and her seed. He shall bruise thy head." That whisper came to man shivering in the presence of his Maker, having nothing more to say by way of excuse; but standing guilty before the Lord. When did the Lord God clothe our parents? Not until first of all He had put the question, "Who told thee that thou wast naked?" Not until the fig-leaves had utterly failed did the Lord bring in the covering skin of the sacrifice, and wrap them in it. If you will pursue the meditation upon the acts of God with men, you will constantly see the same thing. God has given us a wonderful type of salvation in Noah's ark; but Noah was saved in that ark in connection with death; he himself, as it were, immured alive in a tomb, and all the world besides left to destruction. All other hope for Noah was gone, and then the ark rose upon the waters.

Remember the redemption of the children of Israel out of Egypt: it occurred when they were in the saddest plight, and their cry went up to heaven by reason of their bondage. When no arm brought salvation, then with a high hand and an out-stretched arm the Lord brought forth His people. Everywhere before the salvation there comes the humbling of the creature, the overthrow of human hope. As in the back woods of America before there can be tillage, the planting of cities, the arts of civilization, and the transactions of commerce, the woodman's axe must hack and hew: the stately trees of centuries must fall: the roots must be burned, the old reign of nature disturbed. The old must go before the new can come. Even thus the Lord takes away the first, that he may establish the second. The first heaven and the first earth must pass away, or there cannot be a new heaven and a new earth. Now, as it has been outwardly, we ought to expect that it would be the same within us; and when these witherings and fadings occur in our souls, we should only say, "It is the Lord, let him do as seemeth him good."

3. I would have you notice, thirdly, that we are taught in our text *how universally this process is in its range* over the hearts of all those upon whom the Spirit works. The withering is a withering of what? Of part of the flesh and some portion of its tendencies? Nay, observe, "*All* flesh is grass; and *all* the goodli-ness thereof"—the very choice and pick of it—"is as the flower of the field," and what happens to the grass? Does any of it live? "The grass withereth," all of it. The flower, will not that abide? So fair a thing, has not that an immortality? No, it fades: it utterly falls away. So wherever the Spirit of God breathes on the soul of man, there is a withering of everything that is of the flesh, and it is seen that to be carnally minded is death. Of course, we all know and confess that where there is a work of grace, there must be a destruction of our delight in the pleasures of the flesh. When the Spirit of God breathes on us, that which was sweet becomes bitter; that which was bright becomes dim. A man cannot love sin and yet possess the life of God. If he takes pleasure in fleshly joys wherein he once delighted, he is still what he was: he minds the things of the flesh, and therefore he is after the flesh, and he shall die. The world and the lusts thereof are to the unregenerate as beautiful as the meadows in spring, when they are bedecked with flowers, but to the regenerate soul they are a wilderness, a salt land, and not inhabited. Of those very things wherein we once took delight we say, "Vanity of vanities; all is vanity." We cry to be delivered from the poisonous joys of earth, we loathe them, and wonder that we could once riot in them. Beloved hearers, do you know what this kind of withering means? Have you seen the lusts of the flesh, and the pomps and the pleasures

thereof all fade away before your eyes? It must be so, or the Spirit of God has not visited your soul.

But mark, wherever the Spirit of God comes, He destroys the goodliness and flower of the flesh; that is to say, our righteousness withers as our sinfulness. Before the Spirit comes we think ourselves as good as the best. We say, "All these commandments have I kept from my youth up," and we superciliously ask, "What lack I yet?" Have we not been moral? Nay, have we not even been religious? We confess that we may have committed faults, but we think them very venial, and we venture, in our wicked pride, to imagine that, after all, we are not so vile as the word of God would lead us to think. Ah, my dear hearer, when the Spirit of God blows on the comeliness of thy flesh, its beauty will fade as a leaf, and thou wilt have quite another idea of thyself; thou wilt then find no language too severe in which to describe thy past character. Searching deep into thy motives, and investigating that which moved thee to thine actions, thou wilt see so much of evil, that thou wilt cry with the publican, "God be merciful to me, a sinner!"

Where the Holy Ghost has withered up in us our self-righteousness, He has not half completed His work; there is much more to be destroyed yet, and among the rest, away must go our boasted power of resolution. Most people conceive that they can turn to God whenever they resolve to do so. "I am a man of such strength of mind," says one, "that if I made up my mind to be religious, I should be without difficulty." "Ah," saith another volatile spirit, "I believe that one of these days I can correct the errors of the past, and commence a new life." Ah, dear hearers, the resolutions of the flesh are goodly flowers, but they must all fade. When visited by the Spirit of God, we find that even when the will is present with us, how to perform that which we would we find not; yea, and we discover that our will is averse to all that is good, and that naturally we will not come unto Christ that we may have life. What poor frail things resolutions are when seen in the light of God's Spirit!

Still the man will say, "I believe I have, after all, within myself an enlightened conscience and an intelligence that will guide me aright. The light of nature I will use, and I do not doubt that if I wander somewhat I shall find my way back again." Ah, man! thy wisdom, which is the very flower of thy nature, what is it but folly, though thou knowest it not? Unconverted and unrenewed, thou art in God's sight no wiser than the wild ass's colt. I wish thou wert in thine own esteem humbled as a little child at Jesus' feet, and made to cry, "Teach thou me."

When the withering wind of the Spirit moves over the carnal mind, it reveals the death of the flesh in all respects, especially in the matter of power towards that which is good. We then learn that word of our Lord: "Without me ye can do nothing." When I was seeking the Lord, I not only believed that I could not pray without divine help, but I felt in my very soul that I could not. Then I could not even feel aright, or mourn as I would, or groan as I would. I longed to long more after Christ; but, alas ! I could not even feel that I needed Him as I ought to feel it. This heart was then as hard, as adamant, as dead as those that rot in their graves. Oh, what would I at times have given for a tear! I wanted to repent, but could not; longed to believe, but could not; I felt bound, hampered, and paralysed.

This is a humbling revelation of God's Holy Spirit, but a needful one; for the faith of the flesh is not the faith of God's elect. The faith which justifies the soul is the gift of God and not of ourselves. That repentance which is the work of the flesh will need to be repented of. The flower of the flesh must wither; only the seed of the Spirit will produce fruit unto perfection. The heirs of heaven are born not of blood, nor of the will of the flesh, nor of man, but of God. If the work in us be not the Spirit's working, but our own, it will droop and die when most we require its protection; and its end will be as the grass which to-day is, and to-morrow is cast into the oven.

4. You see, then, the universality of this withering work within us, but I beg you also to notice *the completeness of it*. The grass, what does it do? Droop? nay, wither. The flower of the field: what of that? Does it hang its head a little? No, according to Isaiah it fades; and according to Peter it falleth away. There is no reviving it with showers, it has come to its end. Even thus are the awakened led to see that in their flesh there dwelleth no good thing. What dying and withering work some of God's servants have had in their souls! Look at John Bunyan, as he describes himself in his "Grace Abounding!" For how many months and even years was the Spirit engaged in writing death upon all that was the old Bunyan, in order that he might become by grace a new man fitted to track the pilgrims along their heavenly way. We have not all endured the ordeal so long, but in every child of God there must be a death to sin, to the law, and to self, which must be fully accomplished ere he is perfected in Christ and taken to heaven. Corruption cannot inherit incorruption; it is through the Spirit that we mortify the deeds of the body, and therefore live.

But cannot the fleshly mind be improved? By no means; for "the carnal mind is enmity against God: for it is not subject to the law of God, neither indeed can be." Cannot you improve the old nature? No; "ye must be born again." Can it not be taught heavenly things? No. "The natural man receiveth not the things of the Spirit of God: for they are foolishness unto him: neither can he know them, because they are spiritually discerned." There is nothing to be done with the old nature but to let it be laid in the grave; it must be dead, and buried, and when it is so, then the incorruptible seed that liveth and abideth for ever will develop gloriously, the fruit of the new birth will come to maturity, and grace shall be exalted in glory. The old nature never does improve, it is as earthly, and sensual, and devilish in the saint of eighty years of age as it was when first he came to Christ; it is unimproved and unimprovable; towards God it is enmity itself: every imagination of the thoughts of the heart is evil, and that continually. The old nature called "the flesh lusteth against the Spirit, and the Spirit against the flesh: and these are contrary the one to the other," neither can there be peace between them.

5. Let us further notice that all *this withering work in the soul is very painful*. As you read these verses do they not strike you as having a very funereal tone? "All flesh is grass, and all the goodliness thereof is as the flower of the field: the grass withereth, the flower fadeth." This is mournful work, but it must be done. I think those who experience much of it when they first come to Christ have great reason to be thankful. Their course in life will, in all probability, be much brighter and happier, for I have noticed that persons who are converted very easily, and come to Christ with but comparatively little knowledge of their own depravity, have to learn it afterwards, and they remain for a long time babes in Christ, and are perplexed with matters that would not have troubled them if they had experienced a deeper work at first. No, sir; if grace has begun to build in your soul and left any of the old walls of self-trust standing, they will have to come down sooner or later. You may congratulate yourself upon their remaining, but it is a false congratulation, your glorying is not good. I am sure of this, that Christ will never put a new piece upon an old garment, or new wine in old bottles: he knows the rent would be worse in the long run, and the bottles would burst. All that is of nature's spinning must be unravelled. The natural building must come down, lath and plaster, roof and foundation, and we must have a house not made with hands.

It was a great mercy for our city of London that the great fire cleared away all the old buildings which were the lair of the plague, a far healthier city was then built; and it is a great mercy for a man when God sweeps right away all his own righteousness and strength, when He makes him feel that he is nothing and can be nothing, and drives him to confess that

Christ must be all in all, and that his only strength lies in the eternal might of the ever-blessed Spirit.

Observe, brethren, that although this is painful *it is inevitable*. I have already entrenched upon this, and shown you how necessary it is that all of the old should be taken away; but let me further remark that it is inevitable that the old should go, because it is in itself corruptible. Why does the grass wither? Because it is a withering thing. "Its root is ever in its grave, and it must die." How could it spring out of the earth, and be immortal? It is no amaranth: it blooms not in Paradise: it grows in a soil on which the curse has fallen. Every supposed good thing that grows out of your own self, is like yourself, mortal, and it must die. The seeds of corruption are in all the fruits of manhood's tree; let them be as fair to look upon as Eden's clusters, they must decay.

Moreover, it would never do, my brother, that there should be something of the flesh in our salvation and something of the Spirit; for if it were so there would be a division of the honour. Hitherto the praises of God; beyond this my own praises. If I were to win heaven partly through what I had done, and partly through what Christ had done, and if the energy which sanctified me was in a measure my own, and in a measure divine, they that divide the work shall divide the reward, and the songs of heaven while they would be partly to Jehovah must also be partly to the creature. But it shall not be. Down, proud flesh! Down! I say. Though thou cleanse and purge thyself as thou mayst, thou art to the core corrupt; though thou labour unto weariness, thou buildest wood that will be burned, and stubble that will be turned to ashes. Give up thine own self-confidence, and let the work be, and the merit be where the honour shall be, namely, with God alone. It is inevitable, then, that there should be all this withering.

II. Now, let us close with a few sentences concerning THE IMPLANTATION.

According to Peter, although the flesh withers, and the flower thereof falls away, yet in the children of God there is an unwithering something of another kind. "Being born again, not of corruptible seed, but of incorruptible, by the word of God, which liveth and abideth for ever." "The word of the Lord endureth for ever. And this is the word which by the gospel is preached unto you." Now, the gospel is of use to us because it is not of human origin. If it were of the flesh, all it could do for us would not land us beyond the flesh; but the gospel of Jesus Christ is super-human, divine, and spiritual. In its conception it was of God; its great gift, even the Saviour, is a divine gift;

and all its teachings are full of Deity. If you, my hearer, believe
a gospel which you have thought out for yourself, or a philoso-
phical gospel which comes from the brain of man, it is of the flesh,
and will wither, and you will die, and be lost through trusting
in it. The only word that can bless you and be a seed in your
soul must be the living and incorruptible word of the eternal
Spirit.

Now this is the incorruptible word, that "God was made
flesh and dwelt among us"; that "God was in Christ, reconciling
the world unto Himself, not imputing their trespasses unto them."
This is the incorruptible word, that "Whosoever believeth that
Jesus is the Christ is born of God." "He that believeth on Him
is not condemned: but he that believeth not is condemned already
because he hath not believed in the name of the only begotten
Son of God." "God hath given to us eternal life, and this life
is in His Son." Now, brethren, this is the seed; but before it can
grow in your soul, it must be planted there by the Spirit. Do
you receive it this morning? Then the Holy Spirit implants it
in your soul. Do you leap up to it, and say, "I believe it! I
grasp it! On the incarnate God I fix my hope; the substitu-
tionary sacrifice, the complete atonement of Christ is all my
confidence; I am reconciled to God by the blood of Jesus."
Then you possess the living seed within your soul.

And what is the result of it? Why, then there comes, according
to the text, a new life into us, as the result of the indwelling of
the living word, and our being born again by it. A new life it is;
it is not the old nature putting out its better parts; not the old
Adam refining and purifying itself, and rising to something
better. No; have we not said aforetime that the flesh withers
and the flower thereof fades? It is an entirely new life. Ye are
as much new creatures at your regeneration, as if you had never
existed, and had been for the first time created. "Old things are
passed away; behold, all things are become new." The child
of God is beyond and above other men. Other men do not possess
the life which he has received. They are but duplex—body and
soul have they. He is of triple nature—he is spirit, soul, and
body. A fresh principle, a spark of the divine life has dropped
into his soul; he is no longer a natural or carnal man, but he has
become a spiritual man, understanding spiritual things and
possessing a life far superior to anything that belongs to the rest
of mankind. O that God, who has withered in the souls of any
of you that which is of the flesh, may speedily grant you the new
birth through the Word.

Now observe, to close, wherever this new life comes through
the word, it is incorruptible, it lives and abides for ever. To get
the good seed out of a true believer's heart and to destroy the

new nature in him, is a thing attempted by earth and hell, but never yet achieved. Pluck the sun out of the firmament, and you shall not even then be able to pluck grace out of a regenerate heart. It "liveth and abideth for ever," saith the text; it neither can corrupt of itself nor be corrupted. "It sinneth not, because it is born of God." "I give unto them eternal life, and they shall never perish, neither shall any man pluck them out of my hand." "The water that I shall give him shall be in him a well of water springing up into everlasting life." You have a natural life—that will die, it is of the flesh. You have a spiritual life— of that it is written: "Whosoever liveth and believeth in me shall never die." You have now within you the noblest and truest immortality: you must live as God liveth, in peace and joy, and happiness.

But oh, remember, dear hearer, if you have not this "you shall not see life." What then—shall you be annihilated? Ah! no, but "the wrath of the Lord is upon you." You shall exist, though you shall not live. Of life you shall know nothing, for that is the gift of God in Christ Jesus; but of an everlasting death, full of torment and anguish, you shall be the wretched heritor—"the wrath of God abideth on him." You shall be cast into "the lake of fire, which is the second death." You shall be one of those whose "worm dieth not, and whose fire is not quenched." May God, the ever-blessed Spirit, visit you! If He be now striving with you, O quench not His divine flame! Trifle not with any holy thought you have. If this morning you must confess that you are not born again, be humbled by it. Go and seek mercy of the Lord, entreat Him to deal graciously with you and save you. Many who have had nothing but moonlight have prized it, and ere long they have had sunlight.

Above all, remember what the quickening seed is, and reverence it when you hear it preached, "for this is the word which by the gospel is preached unto you." Respect it and receive it. Remember that the quickening seed is all wrapped up in this sentence: "Believe in the Lord Jesus Christ, and thou shalt be saved." "He that believeth and is baptised shall be saved; but he that believeth not shall be damned."

The Lord bless you, for Jesus' sake. Amen.

THE HEAVENLY WIND

A SERMON

Text.—"The wind bloweth where it listeth, and thou hearest the sound thereof, but canst not tell whence it cometh, and whither it goeth: so is every one that is born of the Spirit."—John iii. 8.

THE Holy Spirit is to be admired, not only for the great truths which He teaches us in Holy Scripture, but also for the wonderful manner in which those truths are balanced. The word of God never gives us too much of one thing or too little of another: it never carries a doctrine to an extreme, but tempers it with its corresponding doctrine. Truth seems to run at least in two parallel lines, if not in three, and when the Holy Spirit sets before us one line He wisely points out to us the other. The truth of divine sovereignty is qualified by human responsibility, and the teaching of abounding grace is seasoned by a remembrance of unflinching justice. Scripture gives us as it were the acid and the alkali; the rock and the oil which flows from it; the sword which cuts and the balm which heals. As our Lord sent forth His evangelists two and two so doth He seem to send out His truths two and two, that each may help the other, for the blessing of those who hear them.

Now in this most notable third of John you have two truths taught as plainly as if they were written with a sunbeam, and taught side by side. The one is the necessity of faith in the Lord Jesus Christ, and the fact that whosoever believeth in Him is not condemned. This is a vital doctrine, but the Holy Ghost in this chapter lays equal stress upon the necessity of the new birth or the work of the Holy Spirit, and He states it quite as plainly as the other grand truth. See how they blend—"Ye must be born again"; but "whosoever believeth in him shall not perish, but have everlasting life"; "Except a man be born of water and of the Spirit, he cannot enter into the kingdom of God"; but "he that believeth on him is not condemned." Two great truth are written in letters of light over the gate of heaven, as the requisites of all who enter there—*Reconciliation by the blood of Jesus Christ*; and *Regeneration by the work of the Holy Ghost*. We must not put one of these truths before the other, nor allow one to obliterate or hide the other: they are of equal importance, for they are revealed by the same divine Spirit, and are alike needful to eternal salvation. Faith gives us the rights of the children of God, but the new birth must be experienced that we may have the nature of children: of what use would rights be if we had not the capacity to exercise them?

I. Take the text in reference to THE HOLY SPIRIT HIMSELF. The figure is the wind, and, as most of you know, the Hebrew word for "wind" and for "spirit" is the same; and it is interesting to note that the same is true with the Greek word "*pneuma*," which signifieth both "breath" and "spirit," so that the figure which the Saviour used might very naturally grow out of the word which he employed. The wind is air in motion, and is, of course, material; but air is apparently more spiritual than any of the other elements, except fire, since it is not to be grasped by the hand nor seen with the eye. It is certain that wind really exists, for we hear the sound thereof and observe its various effects, but it is not to be touched, handled or gazed upon; men cannot traffic in it, or measure it in scales, or weigh it in balances. We may watch for hours as we will the clouds as they hasten along like winged fowl, but the wind which driveth them is out of our sight; we observe the waves roused to fury in the tempest, but the breath which so excites them we cannot see. Hence the word becomes all the more excellent a figure of that mighty power, the Holy Ghost, of whose existence no man ever doubts who has come under His influence, but who, nevertheless, is not to be tracked in His movements, nor to be seen as to His divine person; for He is mysterious, incomprehensible, and divine.

First, the wind is a figure of the Holy Ghost in *its freeness*— "The wind bloweth where it listeth." We speak of the wind as the very image of freedom: we say to those who would enthral us, "go bind the winds," as for ourselves we claim to be "free as the winds which roam at their own will." No one can fetter the wind. Xerxes threw chains into the Hellespont to bind the sea, but even he was not fool enough to talk of forging fetters for the winds. The breezes are not to be dictated to. Cæsar may decree what he pleases, but the wind will blow in his face if he looks that way. The Pope may command the gale to change its course, but it will blow around the Vatican neither less nor more for the holy father and the cardinals. A conference of plenipotentiaries from all the powers of Europe may sit for a week and resolve unanimously that the east wind shall not blow for the next six months, but it will take no heed of the arrangement, and will cast dust into the counsellors' eyes, and whistle at their wisdom. No proclamation nor purpose under heaven will be able to affect the wind by so much as half a point of the compass. It will blow according to its own sweet will, where it pleases, when it pleases, how it pleases, and as it pleases, for "the wind bloweth where it listeth."

‣ So is it, only in a far higher and more emphatic sense, with the Holy Spirit, for He is most free and absolute. Ye know that the wind is in the hand of God, and that He ordaineth every zephyr and each tornado: winds arise and tempests blow by order from the throne supreme; but as for the Holy Spirit, He is God Himself, and absolutely free, and worketh according to His own will and pleasure amongst the sons of men.   One nation has been visited by the Holy Spirit and not another—who shall tell me why? Why lie yon heathen lands in the dense darkness while on Britain the light is concentrated?   Why has the Reformation taken root in England and among the northern nations of Europe, while in Spain and Italy it has left scarce a trace?   Why blows the Holy Spirit here and not there?   Is it not that He doeth as He wills? "I will have mercy on whom I will have mercy, and I will have compassion on whom I will have compassion" is the declaration of the divine sovereignty, and the Spirit of God in His movements confirmeth it.

Among the nations where the Spirit of God is at work how is it that He blesseth one man and not another?   How is it that of two men hearing the same sermon, and subject to the same influences at home, one is taken and the other left?   Two children nursed at the same breast, and trained by the same parents, grow up to different ends.   He who perishes in sin has no one to blame but himself, but he who is saved ascribes it all to grace—why came that grace to him?   We never dare to lay the fault of man's not repenting and believing upon God—that resteth with the evil will which refused to obey the gospel; but we dare not ascribe the saving difference in the case of the one who believes to any natural goodness in himself, but we attribute it all to the grace of God, and believe that the Holy Spirit worketh in such to will and to do according to His own good pleasure.   But why works He in us?   Why in any of the chosen?   Ah, why?   "The wind bloweth where it listeth."

So, too, is it with the blessing which rests upon ministries.   One man winneth souls to God, and as a joyous reaper returneth with full sheaves, but another who goeth forth with strong desires, and seems at least to be as earnest as his fellow, comes home with a scanty handful of ears, which he has painfully gleaned.   Why is one man's net full of fish and another's utterly empty?   One servant of the Lord seems, whenever he stands up to preach the gospel, to attract men to Jesus as though he had golden chains in his mouth which he did cast about men's hearts to draw them in joyful captivity to his Lord, while another cries in bitterness of soul, "Who hath believed our report?" Truly, "the wind bloweth where it listeth."

Ay, and these changes happen to each man severally: one day the preacher shall be all alive, his spirit shall be stirred within him, and he shall speak evidently with the Holy Ghost sent down from heaven; and to-morrow he shall find himself dull and heavy, even to his own consciousness, and even more so to his people's experience, for the power rests not upon him. One day he speaketh like the voice of God, and another day he is but as a reed shaken of the wind. His fat kine of years gone by are devoured by the lean cattle of the present. He has his famine as well as his plenty. You shall see him come forth to-day with the unction of the Lord upon him, and his face shining with the glory of fellowship with the Most High, and to-morrow he shall say, "Look not upon me, for I am black," for the glory shall have departed. We know what it is to come forth like Samson when his locks were shorn; and to shake ourselves as at other times and discover that the Lord is not with us. Why all this? Is it not because "the wind bloweth where it listeth?" The Holy Spirit, for His own wise reasons, puts not forth an equal power upon any man at all times. We cannot control nor command the Spirit of the living God: He is in the highest sense a free agent. "Thy free Spirit" is a name which David gave Him, and a most appropriate name it is.

The wind too hath at least in some lands its times and seasons. We know that at certain times of the year we may expect winds, and if they come not to a day or two, yet, as a rule, the month is stormy; and there are also trade winds, monsoons which blow with remarkable regularity and are counted upon by mariners. And so with the Spirit of God. We know that at certain times He visits the churches, and under certain conditions puts forth His power. If, for instance, there is mighty prayer, you may be sure the Spirit of God is at work; if the people of God meet together and besiege the throne of grace with cries and tears, the spiritual barometer indicates that the blessed wind is rising. Besides, the Holy Spirit has graciously connected Himself with two things, truth and prayer. Preach the truth, publish the gospel of Jesus Christ, and it is the habit of the Holy Spirit to make the word quick and powerful to the hearts of men. If we falsify His word if we keep back part of the truth, if we become unfaithful, we cannot expect the Holy Spirit to bless us; but if our teaching be Christ crucified, lovingly set forth, and if the grace of God in its fulness be really declared, the Holy Spirit will attend the truth and make it the great power of God. I will not say that it is always, and without exception so, but I think exceptions must be rare; almost invariably the Spirit beareth witness with the truth in the conversion of men.

So too with prayer, the Holy Spirit is pleased to connect Himself with that also, if it be believing prayer. Here the connection is exceedingly intimate, because it is the Spirit of God who Himself gives the believing prayer, and it is not only true that the Spirit will be given in answer to prayer, but the Spirit is already given or the believing prayer would never have been offered. The spirit of prayerfulness, the spirit of anxiety for the conversion of men is one of the surest indications that the Holy Spirit is already at work in the minds of His people.

Coming back, however, to the great fact that we cannot command the Holy Spirit, what influence ought that truth to have upon us? Should it not be just this? It should lead us to be very tender and jealous in our conduct towards the Holy Ghost, so that we do not grieve Him and cause Him to depart from us. Vex not the Spirit. When you enjoy His gracious operations be devoutly grateful, and walk humbly before God, that you may retain them; and when He is at work let not negligence on your part cause you to receive the grace of God in vain. The wind blew, but the sailor was asleep; it was a favourable breeze, but he had cast anchor and his barque moved not. If he had but known it all through the night he would have spread his sail and have made good headway towards his port; but he slumbered, and the blessed wind whistled through the cordage and the ship lay idle at its moorings. Let it not be so with us. Never suffer the Spirit of God to be with us and find us regardless of His presence.

In the olden times, when country people depended more than they do now on the use of the windmill to grind their corn, some parishes would be half-starved, when week after week there had been no wind. The miller would look up anxiously, and everybody in the parish would become a watchman for his sails, hoping that they would soon be set in motion. If the breeze stirred at the dead of night, and the miller was sound asleep, somebody or other would run and knock him up. "The wind is blowing, the wind is blowing, grind our corn." So it ought to be whenever the Spirit of God is vigorously working in His church, we should eagerly avail ourselves of His power. We should be so anxious for His divine operations that all should be on the watch, so that if some did not discover it others would, and observant ones would cry, "The Holy Ghost is working with us; let us arise and labour more abundantly." Hoist sail when the wind favours; you cannot command it, therefore carefully value it.

But we must pass on. The Holy Spirit is described as being like the wind as to *His manifestations*. "Thou hearest," says Jesus, "the sound thereof." It has been suggested, and some have enlarged upon it, that there are many other manifestations of the presence of wind: you can feel it, you can see its results upon the trees and the waves, and sometimes you can be sure that the wind has been at work by the devastation which it has caused: but in this place our Saviour was not so much alluding to a great wind as to the gentler breezes. The Greek word "*pneuma*" is translated "breath," and can hardly be made to mean a tempest. It was a gentle wind like a zephyr of which the Lord was here speaking. The great winds, as I have already said, can be somewhat calculated upon, but if you sit in the garden in the cool of the evening it is utterly impossible for you to tell whence the zephyrs come and where they go; they are so volatile in their movements and untrackable in their course; here, there, everywhere the soft breezes of evening steal among the flowers. Our Lord tells us that such gentle zephyrs are heard: Nicodemus in the stillness of the night could hear them. "Thou hearest the sound thereof." The leaves rustle, and that is all; you hear a gentle movement of branch and stem, and as it were the tinkling of flower-bells, and so you discover that the wind is flitting among the beds and borders.

Now, beloved, this shows us that the hearing ear is intended by God to be the discerner of the Spirit to men, to the most of men the only discerner that they have. "Thou hearest the sound thereof." What a wonderful dignity the Lord has been pleased to put upon this little organ, the ear. The Romish church gives the preference always to the eye; her priests are always for astonishing men into grace with their wonderful performances; but God's way is "Faith cometh by hearing," and the first detector of the Holy Ghost is the ear. To some men this is the only revealer of His mysterious presence, as I have already said: they hear the sound thereof, that is to say, they hear the gospel preached, they hear the word of God read. Truth when it is couched in words is the rustling of the holy wind, it is the footstep of the Eternal Spirit as mysteriously He passes along a congregation. Oh, what grief it is that some never get any further than this, but abide where Nicodemus was at the first: they hear the sound thereof and nothing more. Some of you are now daily hearing truth which has saved thousands, but it does not save you; you are hearing the very truth which peoples heaven, but yet it leaves you without a hope of eternal life; yet be ye sure of this, the kingdom of God has come nigh unto you. "Thou hearest the sound thereof," and that wind whose whispers you hear is not far off thine own cheek. When thou hearest the rustling amongst the boughs of the trees the breezes are not far to seek, nor is the Spirit of God far away when His sound is heard.

Some hearers, however, go further, for they hear the sound of the Spirit in their consciences and it disturbs them; they would sleep as do others, but as the wind sometimes comes whistling through the keyhole or howls down the chimney and wakes the sluggard, or if the man be lying in a garden asleep the breezes play around his ears and face and startle him, so is it with many unconverted people; they cannot be quiet, for they hear the sound of the Holy Spirit in their consciences, and are troubled and perplexed. There is a revival and they are not saved, but they are startled and alarmed by it; their sister is converted, they are not, but still it comes very near them, and they feel as if an arrow had gone whizzing by their own ear. It is hard living in a careless state in the midst of revival. "Thou hearest the sound thereof." But some of you in your conscience are hearing the sound now in your family circle, from the fact that one after another of your relatives have been brought to know the Lord; you cannot avoid feeling that there is something powerful abroad, though it has not yet exerted its regenerating power upon you.

As for the man who is saved, he hears the Holy Spirit in the most emphatic sense, and with what variety that sound comes to him. At first he heard it as a threatening wind, which bowed him in sadness and seemed to sweep all his hopes to the ground, as the sere leaves of the forest are carried in the autumn's wind. When the Spirit's voice sounded in mine ears at the first it was as a wail of woe, as a wind among the tombs, as a sigh among faded lilies. It seemed as if all my hopes were puffed away like smoke, or as the night mists in the morning breeze; nothing was left me but to mourn my nothingness. Then I heard a sound as of the hot sirocco of the East, as if it issued from a burning oven. You know the text, "The grass withereth and the flower thereof fadeth away because the Spirit of the Lord bloweth upon it: surely the people is grass." In my soul there had bloomed a fair meadow of golden kingcups and fair flowers of many dainty colours, but the Spirit of God blew there on and withered it all, and left it as a dry, brown, rusty plain, whereon was neither life nor comeliness. So far the sacred wind destroys that which is evil, but it ends not there, for we thank God we have heard the sound of the Spirit as a quickening wind. The prophet cried, "Come from the four winds, O breath, and breathe upon these slain that they may live"; the wind came and the dead arose an exceeding great army.

The like miracle has been wrought on us. The sere bones of our own death have crept together, bone unto His bone, and flesh has come upon them, and now because of the divine breath we have begun to live. Now, also, when the Holy Spirit visits us He renews our life and energy, and we have life more abundantly. The Holy Spirit has since then been to us full often a melting wind, "He causeth His wind to blow and the waters flow." Locked up in the chains of ice all through the winter the waters are still as a stone, but the spring-winds come, the brooklets find liberty and leap away to the rivers, and the rivers flow in all their free force to add their volume to the sea. So hath the Spirit of God oftentimes broken up our frost, and given our spirits joyous liberty. He melts the rocky heart and dissolves the iron spirit, at the sound of His goings men are moved to feeling.

We know the sound of this wind as a diffusive breath, drawing forth and diffusing our slumbering graces. "Awake, O north wind; and come, thou south; blow upon my garden, that the spices thereof may flow out." Oh, what a sweet unloosing of holy gratitude, and love, and hope, and joy has there been in our heart when the Spirit of God has visited us. As sweet essences lie hidden in the flowers, and come not forth until the loving wind doth entice them to fly abroad, so do sweet graces lie within renewed spirits until the Holy Ghost cometh and speaketh to them, and they know his voice and come forth to meet him, and so sweet fragrances are shed abroad.

Yes, my brethren, all this we know, and we have heard the sound of the Holy Spirit in another sense, namely, as going forth with us to the battle of the Lord. We have heard that sound of a going in the tops of the mulberry trees which David heard, and we have bestirred ourselves, and victory has been ours. If we have not heard that rushing mighty wind which came at Pentecost, yet have we felt its divine effect, which ceaseth not, but still bringeth life, power, energy, and all that is wanted for the conversion of the sons of men to us who are bidden to go forth and preach the gospel amongst the nations. In all these respects the Holy Ghost has manifested Himself, as wind does, by His sound. "Thou hearest the sound thereof." "Their sound went into all the earth and their words unto the ends of the world."

A third likeness of the Spirit to the wind is set before us in the point of *mystery*. "Thou canst not tell whence it cometh nor whither it goeth." Of the wind we may tell that it comes from such and such a quarter or point, but you cannot put your finger on the map and say, "The north wind began in this region," or "here the west wind was born." Indeed, we know very little about the winds, their origin, or their laws. One of the best and most accurate observers of the wind during thirty years recorded every wind in his region, until at the end of the term he abandoned the few rules which he had laid down during the first two or three years, for he found that no rule held good. No man can say whence the wind leapeth forth. The heathen dreamed of a certain cave wherein the winds were enclosed as in a prison, and suffered to go abroad one by one: it was but a fable; we know not where the winds first spread their wings, or where they sleep when all is still. So is it with the Holy Spirit in the mind of man, His first movements are hidden in mystery.

You know that you are converted, my dear friend, and you know somewhere about the time, and probably you remember

somewhat as to the means which the Lord used for your salvation.
Those outward circumstances you do know, but how the Holy
Spirit operated upon you, you do not and cannot tell any more
than you can tell how swells the life within the seed until it springs
up and becomes the full corn in the ear, or how the sap in the
trees first descendeth in the winter and afterwards climbeth again
in the spring.   There are secrets which nature doth not reveal,
and the work of the Spirit is even more a secret, and assuredly
no man can explain it to his fellow or to himself.   Why is it,
my friend, that you obtained a blessing under one sermon but
not under another, and yet when you spoke to your sister she had
been more blessed under the second than the first?   The power
does not come from the preacher, then, it is clear, and "thou
canst not tell whence it cometh,"

There are times in which you feel not only that you can pray
but that you must pray; how come you to be in that state?   I
know what it is to feel in a very ecstacy of delight in the Lord,
for which I can scarcely account, for at another time when I
have been engaged in the same work, and I think with the same
earnestness, I have not been conscious of any such exceeding
delight in God.   At one time the heart will be full of penitence
as if it would break for sin, and at another season it will overflow
with such delight in Christ that the sin seems almost forgotten
in the pardoning sacrifice.   Why these diverse operations ?

We know what it is at times to feel such a sense of death upon
us as to be earnestly preparing for our last hours; and at another
time to be altogether forgetful of death, and to be living, as it
were, the immortal life already, raised up together and made to
sit together with Christ.   But how these various modes and forms
and workings of the Spirit come who among us shall tell?   Go
trace the dewdrops, if ye can, to the womb of the morning, and
discover which way went the lightning's flash, or how the thunder
rolled along the mountain tops, but ye cannot tell nor can you
guess whence cometh the Spirit of God into your souls.

Nor can we tell whither it goeth.   Here, again, is another
mystery.   Oh, it charms me to think that when we let loose the
truth in the power of the Spirit we never know where it will
fly.   A child takes a seed, one of those downy seeds which has
its own parachute to bear it through the air; the little one blows
it into the air, but who knows where that downy seed shall settle,
and in whose garden it shall grow?   Such is truth, even from the
mouths of babes and sucklings.   Whole continents have been
covered with strange flowers simply by the wind wafting foreign
seeds thither, and mariners have discovered sunny islets out there
in the Southern Sea, where foot of man has never trodden,
covered with abundance of vegetation which the wind has by

degrees wafted thither. Scatter the truth on all sides, for you cannot tell where the Spirit will carry it. Fling it to the winds, and you shall find it after many days. Scatter the living seed with both hands, send it north, south, east and west, and God will give it wings,

> " Waft, waft ye winds the story,
>   And you, ye waters roll,
>   Till like a sea of glory
>   It spreads from pole to pole."

I had a letter but the other day when I was sore sick: it was written by a sister in Christ in the very heart of the empire of Brazil. She said that she had met with a copy of my "Morning Readings," and had found thereby the way of peace, and, therefore, she wrote me such a loving, touching letter, that, as I read it, it brought tears to my eyes. There was something more affecting yet, for at the end was written in another hand, some words to the effect that his dear wife who had written the above letter had died soon after finishing it, and with a bleeding heart the lone husband sent it on to me, rejoicing that ever the word came to his wife's soul in the far-off land.

Brethren, you do not know where the word will go and the Spirit with it. In Bohemia the papists thought they had stamped out the gospel, and with cruel edicts they kept down all thought of Protestanism, but just lately, since the toleration, the gospel has been preached in that country, and to the surprise of everybody there have come forward men and women from lone cottages in the woods and from different corners of the great cities of Bohemia, bringing with them ancient copies of the word of God, themselves being eager to know the precious truth for which they remember that their fathers died. A truth will go adown the centuries: like the river, it sings

> " Men may come and men may go,
>   But I go on for ever."

"Thou canst not tell whither it goeth," it will travel on till the millennium. Send that saying abroad that the truth cannot die. The persecutor cannot kill it, it is immortal, like the God who sent it forth; the persecutor cannot even stay its course, it is divine. Popery will always be in danger so long as there is one leaf of the Bible upon earth, or one man living who knows the Saviour. Antichrist cannot triumph; the Holy Spirit wars against it with the sword of the word, and thou canst not tell how far into the heart of error any truth may be driven. To the overthrow of falsehood and the death of sin the Spirit speeds on, but thou knowest not how.

"Thou canst not tell whither it goeth" either in any one heart. If you have received the Holy Spirit into your heart, you cannot tell whither He will carry you. I am sure that William Carey, when he gave his young heart to Christ never thought the Spirit of God would carry him to Serampore to preach the gospel to the Hindoos; and when George Whitefield first drank of the life-giving spirit it never occurred to him that the pot-boy at the Bell Inn at Gloucester would thunder the gospel over two continents and turn thousands to Christ. No! You know not to what blessed end this wind will waft you. Commit yourselves to it: be not disobedient to the heavenly vision; be ready to be borne along as the Spirit of God shall help you, even as the dust in the summer's breeze. And O child of God, you do not yourself know to what heights of holiness and degrees of knowledge and ecstasies of enjoyment the Spirit of God will bear you. "Eye hath not seen nor ear heard the things which God hath prepared for them that love Him," and though He hath revealed them by His Spirit (for the Spirit searcheth all things, even the deep things of God), yet even to the best taught child of God it is not yet known to the full whither the Spirit of God goeth. "Trust ye in the Lord for ever, for in the Lord Jehovah there is everlasting strength," and He will bear you onward and upward, even to perfection itself, and you shall be with Jesus, where He is, and behold His glory.

II. I have but a few minutes left for my second head, but I do not need many, since I do not wish to say much upon it. The text relates to THOSE WHO ARE BORN OF THE SPIRIT. "The wind bloweth where it listeth, and thou hearest the sound thereof, but canst not tell whence it cometh, and whither it goeth: so is every one that is born of the Spirit." The birth partakes of the natures of the parent. That which is born of the Spirit is like unto the Spirit of which it is born, even as that which is born of the flesh is flesh, and is similar to the flesh by which it is begotten. The twice-born man is like the Holy Ghost who produced him, and he is like Him in each of the points which we have already dwelt upon.

As to *freedom*, you may say of Him, "He bloweth where He listeth." The Spirit of God makes the believer a free man, bestows on him the freedom of His will which he never had before, and gives him a delightful consciousness of liberty. "If the Son make you free ye shall be free indeed." I do not affirm that every spiritual man does as he lists, because, alas, I see another law in our members warring against the law of our mind, and bringing us into captivity to the law of sin and death: but still, "where the Spirit of the Lord is, there is liberty."

Now you can pray, which you could not do before; now you can praise, though you could not extract a note of praise from your ungrateful heart before; now you can cry, "Abba, Father"; now you can draw near to God. You are no longer under man's control, you blow where you list; you are not now ruled by priestcraft, nor domineered over by the opinion of your fellow-man. The Lord has set you free, and you list to go where God's word bids you go, and you find the utmost liberty in going that way. Oh, brethren, I cannot tell you the change which is felt by a regenerate man in the matter of spiritual liberty. When you were under the bondage of the law, of custom and of sin, and of fear of death and dread of hell, you were like a man shut up in one of those cells in Venice which lie below the level of the water mark, where the air is foul, and the poor prisoner can only stir half-a-dozen feet and then walk back again in the darkness; but when the Spirit of God comes He brings the soul from darkness into light, from clammy damp into the open air; He sets before you an open door, He helps you to run in the way of God's commands, and as if that were not enough, He even lends you wings, and bids you mount as the eagle, for He has set you free.

Again, the man who is born of the Spirit is somewhat *manifested;* and is known by his sound. "Thou hearest the sound thereof." The most ungodly man if he lives near a Christian will hear the sound of him. The secret life within will speak; words there will be, for Christians are not dumb, but actions will speak more loudly still; and even apart from actions the very spirit and tone of the man who is really regenerated will speak, and the ungodly man will be compelled to hear it. "Thou hearest the sound thereof."

And now notice *the mystery* there is about a Christian. Thou knowest nothing, if thou art unregenerate, about the life the believer leads, for he is dead, and his life is hid with Christ in God. Thou knowest not whence he cometh forth in the morning; those beds of spices which have made his garments fragrant thou hast not seen; that weeping in prayer or that rejoicing in fellow-ship with which he opened the morning thou knowest nothing of, and thou canst not know until thou art thyself born of the Spirit. Neither canst thou tell whither the spiritual man goeth. In the midst of his trouble thou seest him calm; dost thou know where he went to win that rare quietude? In the hour of death thou seest him triumphant; dost thou know where he has been to learn to die so joyously? No, the unregenerate man knows not whither the believer goes. There is a secret place of the Most High, and they shall abide under the shadow of the Almighty who have once learned to enter there, but carnal men come not into this secret chamber.

The Christian life is a mystery all through, from its beginning to its end: to the worldling all a mystery; and to the Christian himself a puzzle. He cannot read his own riddle, nor understand himself. This one thing he knoweth, "Whereas I was once blind, now I see"; this also he knoweth, "O Lord, I am thy servant, I am thy servant, and the son of thine handmaid: thou hast loosed my bonds"; this also he knoweth, that when his Lord shall be revealed then will he also shine forth as the sun. The life within him in its coming and going is all a mystery to him, but he blesses God that he has fellowship therein. He goes on his way feeling that though men know not whence he is, nor whither he is going, yet the Lord knows him, and he himself is sure that he is going to his Father and his God. O that every one of you had so delightful a hope. The Lord grant it to you, for Jesus's sake.

THE PENTECOSTAL WIND AND FIRE

A Sermon

Text.—"And suddenly there came a sound from heaven as of a rushing mighty wind, and it filled all the house where they were sitting. And there appeared unto them cloven tongues like as of fire, and it sat upon each of them. And they were all filled with the Holy Ghost, and began to speak with other tongues, as the Spirit gave them utterance."—Acts ii. 2–4.

From the descent of the Holy Ghost at the beginning we may learn something concerning His operations at the present time. Remember at the outset that whatever the Holy Spirit was at the first that He is now, for as God He remaineth for ever the same: whatsoever He then did He is able to do still, for His power is by no means diminished. As saith the prophet Micah, "O thou that art named the house of Jacob, is the spirit of the Lord straitened?" We should greatly grieve the Holy Spirit if we supposed that His might was less to-day than in the beginning. Although we may not expect, and need not desire, the miracles which came with the gift of the Holy Spirit, so far as they were physical, yet we may both desire and expect that which was intended and symbolized by them, and we may reckon to see the like spiritual wonders performed among us at this day.

Pentecost, according to the belief of the Jews, was the time of the giving of the law; and if when the law was given there was a marvellous display of power on Sinai, it was to be expected that when the gospel was given, whose ministration is far more glorious, there should be some special unveiling of the divine presence. If at the commencement of the gospel we behold the Holy Spirit working great signs and wonders may we not expect a continuance —nay, if anything, an increased display—of His power as the ages roll on? The law vanished away, but the gospel will never vanish; it shineth more and more to the perfect millennial day; therefore, I reckon that, with the sole exception of physical miracles, whatever was wrought by the Holy Ghost at the first we may look to be wrought continually while the dispensation lasts. It ought not to be forgotten that Pentecost was the feast of first fruits; it was the time when the first ears of ripe corn were offered unto God. If, then, at the commencement of the gospel harvest we see so plainly the power of the Holy Spirit, may we not most properly expect infinitely more as the harvest advances and most of all when the most numerous sheaves shall be ingathered? May we not conclude that if the Pentecost was thus marvellous the actual harvest will be more wonderful still?

This morning my object is not to talk of the descent of the Holy Spirit as a piece of history, but to view it as a fact bearing upon us at this hour, even upon us who are called in these latter days to bear our testimony for the truth. The Father hath sent us the Comforter that He may dwell in us till the coming of the Lord. The Holy Ghost has never returned, for He came in accordance with the Saviour's prayer, to abide with us for ever. The gift of the Comforter was not temporary, and the display of His power was not to be once seen and no more. The Holy Ghost is here, and we ought to respect His divine working among us: and if He does not so work we should search ourselves to see what it is that hindereth, and whether there may not be somewhat in ourselves which vexes Him, so that He restrains His sacred energy, and doth not work among us as He did aforetime. May God grant that the meditation of this morning may increase our faith in the Holy Ghost, and inflame our desires towards Him, so that we may look to see Him fulfilling His mission among men as at the beginning.

I. First, I shall call your attention to THE INSTRUCTIVE SYMBOLS of the Holy Spirit, which were made prominent at Pentecost. They were two. There was a sound as of a rushing mighty wind, and there were cloven tongues as it were of fire.

Take the symbols separately. The first is *wind*—an emblem of Deity, and therefore a proper symbol of the Holy Spirit. Often under the Old Testament God revealed Himself under the emblem of breath or wind: indeed, as most of you know, the Hebrew word for "wind" and "spirit" is the same. So, with the Greek word, when Christ talked to Nicodemus, it is not very easy for translators to tell us when He said "spirit" and when He said "wind"; indeed, some most correctly render the original all the way through by the word "wind," while others with much reason have also used the word "spirit" in their translation. The original word signified either the one or the other, or both. Wind is, of all material things, one of the most spiritual in appearance; it is invisible, ethereal, mysterious; hence, men have fixed upon it as being nearest akin to spirit. In Ezekiel's famous vision, when he saw the valley full of dry bones, we all know that the Spirit of God was intended by that vivifying wind which came when the prophet prophesied and blew upon the withered relics till they were quickened into life. "The Lord hath His way in the whirlwind," thus He displays Himself when He works: "The Lord answered Job out of the whirlwind," thus He reveals Himself when He teaches His servants.

Observe that this wind was on the day of Pentecost accompanied with a sound—a sound as of a rushing mighty wind; for albeit the Spirit of God can work in silence, yet in saving operations He frequently uses sound. I would be the last to depreciate meetings in which there is nothing but holy silence, for I could wish that we had more reverence for silence, and it is in stillness that the inner life is nourished; yet the Holy Ghost does not work for the advancement of the kingdom of God by silence alone, for faith cometh by hearing. There is a sound as of a rushing, mighty wind, when the word is sounded forth throughout whole nations by the publishing of the gospel. The sound came on this occasion, no doubt, to call the attention of the assembly to what was about to occur, to arouse them, and to fill them with awe! There is something indescribably solemn about the rush of a rising tempest; it bows the soul before the sublime mystery of divine power. What more fitting as an attendant upon divine working than the deeply solemn rush of a mighty wind.

With this awe-inspiring sound as of a mighty wind, there was clear indication of its coming from heaven. Ordinary winds blow from this or that quarter of the skies, but this descended from heaven itself: it was distinctly like a down-draught from above. This sets forth the fact that the true Spirit, the Spirit of God, neither comes from this place nor that neither can His power be controlled or directed by human authority, but His working is ever from above, from God Himself. The work of the Holy Spirit is, so to speak, the breath of God, and His power is evermore in a special sense the immediate power of God. Coming downward, therefore, this mysterious wind passed into the chamber where the disciples were assembled, and filled the room. An ordinary rushing mighty wind would have been felt outside the room, and would probably have destroyed the house or injured the inmates, if it had been aimed at any one building; but this heavenly gust filled but did not destroy the room, it blessed but did not overthrow the waiting company.

The meaning of the symbol is that as breath, air, wind, is the very life of man, so is the Spirit of God the life of the spiritual man. By Him are we quickened at the first; by Him are we kept alive afterwards; by Him is the inner life nurtured, and increased, and perfected. The breath of the nostrils of the man of God is the Spirit of God.

This holy breath was not only intended to quicken them, but to invigorate them. They took in great draughts of heavenly life; they felt animated, aroused, and bestirred. A sacred enthusiasm came upon them, because they were filled with the Holy Ghost; and, girt with that strength, they rose into a nobler form of life than they had known before.

No doubt this wind was intended to show the irresistible power of the Holy Ghost; for simple as the air is, and mobile and apparently feeble, yet set it in motion, and you feel that a thing of life is among you; make that motion more rapid, and who knows the power of the restless giant who has been awakened. See, it becomes a storm, a tempest, a hurricane, a tornado, a cyclone. Nothing can be more potent than the wind when it is thoroughly roused, and so, though the Spirit of God be despised among men, so much so that they do not even believe in His existence, yet let Him work with the fulness of His power, and you will see what He can do. He comes softly, breathing like a gentle zephyr, which fans the flowers, but does not dislodge the insect of most gauzy wing, and our hearts are comforted. He comes like a stirring breeze, and we are quickened to a livelier diligence: our sails are hoisted and we fly before the gale. He comes with yet greater strength, and we prostrate ourselves in the dust as we hear the thunder of His power, bringing down with a crash false confidences and refuges of lies! How the firm reliances of carnal men, which seemed to stand like rocks, are utterly cast down! How men's hopes, which appeared to be rooted like oaks, are torn up by the roots before the breath of the convincing Spirit! What can stand against Him? Oh! that we did but see in these latter days something of that mighty rushing wind which breaketh the cedars of Lebanon, and sweeps before it all things that would resist its power.

The second Pentecostal symbol was *fire*. Fire, again, is a frequent symbol of Deity. Abraham saw a burning lamp, and Moses beheld a burning bush. When Solomon had builded his holy and beautiful house, its consecration lay in the fire of God descending upon the sacrifice to mark that the Lord was there; for when the Lord had dwelt aforetime in the tabernacle, which was superseded by the temple, He revealed Himself in a pillar of cloud by day and a pillar of fire by night. "Our God is a consuming fire." Hence the symbol of fire is a fit emblem of God the Holy Spirit. Let us adore and worship Him. Tongues of flame sitting on each man's head betoken a personal visitation to the mind and heart of each one of the chosen company. Not to consume them came the fires, for no one was injured by the flaming tongue; to men whom the Lord has prepared for His approach there is no danger in His visitations. They see God, and their lives are preserved; they feel His fires, and are not consumed. This is the privilege of those alone who have been prepared and purified for such fellowship with God.

The intention of the symbol was to show them that the Holy Spirit would illuminate them, as fire gives light. "He shall lead you into all truth." Henceforth they were to be no more children untrained, but to be teachers in Israel, instructors of the nations whom they were to disciple unto Christ: hence the

Spirit of light was upon them. But fire doth more than give light: it inflames; and the flames which sat upon each showed them that they were to be ablaze with love, intense with zeal, burning with self-sacrifice; and that they were to go forth among men to speak not with the chill tongue of deliberate logic, but with burning tongues of passionate pleading; persuading and entreating men to come unto Christ that they might live. The fire signified inspiration. God was about to make them speak under a divine influence, to speak as the Spirit of God should give them utterance. Oh! blessed symbol, would God that all of us experienced its meaning to the full and that the tongue of fire did sit upon every servant of the Lord. May a fire burn steadily within to destroy our sin, a holy sacrificial flame to make us whole burnt offerings unto God, a never-dying flame of zeal for God, and devotion to the cross.

Note that the emblem was not only fire, but a tongue of fire; for God meant to have a speaking church: not a church that would fight with the sword—with that weapon we have nought to do—but a church that should have a sword proceeding out of its mouth, whose one weapon should be the proclamation of the gospel of Jesus Christ. I should think from what I know of some preachers that when they had their Pentecost the influence sat upon them in the form of tongues of flowers; but the apostolic Pentecost knew not flowers, but flames. What fine preaching we have nowadays! What new thoughts, and poetical turns! This is not the style of the Holy Ghost. Soft and gentle is the flow of smooth speech which tells of the dignity of man, the grandeur of the century, the toning down of all punishment for sin, and the probable restoration of all lost spirits, including the arch-fiend himself. This is the Satanic ministry, subtle as the serpent, bland as his seducing words to Eve.

The Holy Ghost calls us not to this mode of speech. Fire, intensity, zeal, passion as much as you will, but as for aiming at effect by polished phrases and brilliant periods—these are fitter for those who would deceive men than for those who would tell them the message of the Most High. The style of the Holy Ghost is one which conveys the truth to the mind in the most forcible manner,—it is plain but flaming, simple but consuming. The Holy Spirit has never written a cold period throughout the whole Bible, and never did He speak by a man a lifeless word, but evermore He gives and blesses the tongue of fire.

These, then, are the two symbols:—He comes as the wind, which wafts the words we speak, and as fire which burns a way for the truth we utter. Our words are now full of life and flame; they are borne by the breath of the Spirit, and they fall like fire-flakes, and set the souls of men blazing with desire after God. If the Holy Spirit shall rest upon me or upon you, or upon any of us, to qualify us for service, it shall be after this fashion—not merely of life for ourselves, but of fiery energy in dealing with others.   Come on us even now, O rushing mighty wind and tongue of fire, for the world hath great need.   It lies stagnant in the malaria of sin and needs a healing wind; it is shrouded in dreadful night, and needs the flaming torch of truth.   There is neither health nor light for it but from Thee, O blessed Spirit; come, then, upon it through Thy people.

Now put these two symbols together; only mind what you are at. Wind and fire together!   I have kept them separate in my discourse hitherto; and you have seen power in each one; what are they together?   Rushing mighty wind alone how terrible! Who shall stand against it?   See how the gallant ships dash together, and the monarchs of the forest bow their heads.   And fire alone!   Who shall stand against it when it devours its prey? But set wind and fire to work in hearty union!   Remember the old city of London.   When first the flames began it was utterly impossible to quench them because the wind fanned the flame, and the buildings gave way before the fire-torrent.   O God, send us the Holy Ghost in this fashion: give us both the breath of spiritual life and the fire of unconquerable zeal, till nation after nation shall yield to the sway of Jesus.   O Thou who art our God, answer us by fire, we pray Thee.   Answer us both by wind and fire, and then shall we see to be God indeed.   The kingdom comes not, and the work is flagging.   O that Thou wouldest send the wind and the fire!   Thou wilt do this when we are all of one accord, all believing, all expecting, all prepared by prayer. Lord, bring us to this waiting state.

II.   Secondly, my brethren, follow me while I call your attention to THE IMMEDIATE EFFECTS of this descent of the Holy Spirit, for these symbols were not sent in vain.   There were two immediate effects: the first was *filling*, and the second was *the gift of utterance*. I call special attention to the first, namely, filling: "It filled all the house where they were sitting": and it did not merely fill the house, but the man—"They were all filled with the Holy Ghost."   When they stood up to speak even the ribald mockers in the crowd noticed this, for they said, "These men are full," and though they added "with new wine," yet they evidently detected a singular fulness about them.   We are poor, empty things by nature, and useless while we remain so: we need to be filled with the Holy Ghost.   Where the Spirit of God is truly at work He first fills and then gives utterance: that is His way. Oh that you and I were at this moment filled with the Holy

Ghost. "Full!" Then they were not cold, and dead, and empty of life as we sometimes are. "Full." Then there was no room for anything else in any one of them! They were too completely occupied by the heavenly power to have room for the desires of the flesh. Fear was banished, every minor motive was expelled: the Spirit of God as it flooded their very being drove out of them everything that was extraneous. They had many faults and many infirmities before, but that day, when they were filled with the Spirit of God, faults and infirmities were no more perceptible. They became different men from what they had ever been before: men full of God are the reverse of men full of self. Out of a full church the world shall receive salvation, but never out of an empty one. The first thing we want as a church is to be filled with the Holy Ghost: the gift of utterance will then come as a matter of course.

The next Pentecostal symbol was *utterance*. As soon as the Spirit of God filled them they began to speak at once. It seems to me that they began to speak before the people had come together. They could not help it; the inner forces demanded expression, and they must speak. So when the Spirit of God really comes upon a man, He does not wait till He has gathered an audience of the size which He desires, but He seizes the next opportunity. He speaks to one person, He speaks to two, He speaks to three, to anybody: He must speak, for He is full, and must have vent.

When the Spirit of God fills a man He speaks so as to be understood. The crowd spake different languages, and these Spirit-taught men spoke to them in the language of the country in which they were born. This is one of the signs of the Spirit's utterance. If my friend over yonder talks in a Latinized style to a company of costermongers, I will warrant you the Holy Ghost has nothing to do with him. If a learned brother fires over the heads of his congregation with a grand oration, he may trace his elocution, if he likes, to Cicero and Demosthenes, but do not let him ascribe it to the Holy Spirit, for that is not after His manner. The Spirit of God speaks so that His words may be understood, and if there be any obscurity it lies in the language used by the Lord Himself.

The crowd not only understood, but they felt. There were lancets in this Pentecostal preaching, and the hearers "were pricked in the heart." The truth wounded men, and the slain of the Lord were many, for the wounds were in the most vital part. They could not make it out: they had heard speakers before, but this was quite a different thing. The men spake fire-flakes, and one hearer cried to his fellow, "What is this?" The preachers were speaking flame, and the fire dropped into the hearts of men till they were amazed and confounded.

Those are the two effects of the Holy Spirit,—a fulness of the Spirit in the ministry and the church, and next, a fire ministry, and a church on fire, speaking so as to be felt and understood by those around. Causes produce effects like themselves, and this wind and fire ministry soon did its work. We read that this "was noised abroad." Of course it was, because there had been a noise as of a rushing mighty wind. Next to that we read that all the people came together, and were confounded. There was naturally a stir, for a great wind from heaven was rushing. All were amazed and astonished, and while some enquired believingly, others began to mock. Of course they did: there was a fire burning, and fire is a dividing thing, and this fire began to separate between the precious and the vile, as it always will do when it comes into operation. We may expect at the beginning of a true revival to observe a movement among the people, a noise, and a stir. These things are not done in a corner. Cities will know of the presence of God, and crowds will be attracted by the event.

This was the immediate effect of the Pentecostal marvel, and I shall now ask you to follow me to my third point, which is this:—

III.   The Holy Spirit being thus at work, what was THE MOST PROMINENT SUBJECT which these full men began to preach about with words of fire? Suppose that the Holy Spirit should work mightily in the church, what would our ministers preach about? "We do hear them speak in our own tongues the wonderful works of God." Their subject was the wonderful works of God. Oh, that this might be to my dying day my sole and only topic,—"The wonderful works of God." For, first, they spoke of *redemption*, that wonderful work of God. Peter's sermon was a specimen of how they spoke of it. He told the people that Jesus was the Son of God, that they had crucified and slain Him, but that He had come to redeem men, and that there was salvation through His precious blood. He preached redemption. Oh, how this land will echo again and again with "Redemption, redemption, redemption, redemption by the precious blood," when the Holy Ghost is with us. This is fit fuel for the tongue of flame: this is something worthy to be wafted by the divine wind. "God was in Christ, reconciling the world unto himself, not imputing their trespasses unto them." "The blood of Jesus Christ his Son cleanseth us from all sin." This is one of the wonderful works of God of which we can never make too frequent mention.

They certainly spoke of the next wonderful work of God, namely, *regeneration*. There was no concealing of the work of the Holy Spirit in that primitive ministry. It was brought to the front. Peter said, "Ye shall receive the Holy Ghost." The preachers of Pentecost told of the Spirit's work by the Spirit's power: conversion, repentance, renewal, faith, holiness, and such things were freely spoken of and ascribed to their real author, the divine Spirit. If the Spirit of God shall give us once again a full and fiery ministry we shall hear it clearly proclaimed, "Ye must be born again," and we shall see a people forthcoming which are born, not of blood, nor of the will of the flesh, but of the will of God, and by the energy which cometh from heaven. A Holy Ghost ministry cannot be silent about the Holy Ghost and His sacred operations upon the heart.

And very plainly they spoke on a third wonderful work of God, namely, *remission* of sin. This was the point that Peter pushed home to them, that on repentance they should receive remission of sins. What a blessed message is this;—Pardon for crimes of deepest dye, a pardon bought with Jesus' blood, free pardon, full pardon, irreversible pardon given to the vilest of the vile when they ground their weapons of rebellion, and bow at the feet that once were nailed to the tree. If we would prove ourselves to be under divine influence, we must keep to the divine message of fatherly forgiveness to returning prodigals. What happier word can we deliver?

These are the doctrines which the Holy Ghost will revive in the midst of the land when He worketh mightily—redemption, regeneration, remission. If you would have the Spirit of God resting on your labours, dear brothers and sisters, keep these three things ever to the front, and make all men hear in their own tongue the wonderful works of God.

IV. I shall close by noticing, in the fourth place, what were the GLORIOUS RESULTS of all this. Have patience with me, if you find the details somewhat long. The result of the Spirit coming as wind and fire, filling and giving utterance, was, first, in the hearers' *deep feeling*. There was never, perhaps, in the world such a feeling excited by the language of mortal man as that which was aroused in the crowds in Jerusalem on that day. You might have seen a group here, and a group there, all listening to the same story of the wondrous works of God, and all stirred and affected; for the heavenly wind and fire went with the preaching, and they could not help feeling its power. We are told that they were pricked in the heart. They had painful emotions, they felt wounds which killed their enmity. The word struck at the centre of their being: it pierced the vital point.

Alas, people come into our places of worship nowadays to hear the preacher, and their friends ask them on their return, "How did you like him?" Was that your errand, to see how you liked him? What practical benefit is there in such a mode of using the servants of God? Are we sent among you to give opportunities for criticism? Yet the mass of men seem to think that we are nothing better than fiddlers or play-actors, who come upon the stage to help you while away an hour. O my hearers, if we are true to our God, and true to you, ours is a more solemn business than most men dream. The object of all true preaching is the heart: we aim at divorcing the heart from sin, and wedding it to Christ. Our ministry has failed, and has not the divine seal set upon it, unless it makes men tremble, makes them sad, and then anon brings them to Christ, and causes them to rejoice.

Then followed an *earnest enquiry*. "They were pricked in their heart, and they said to Peter and the rest of the apostles, Men and brethren, what shall we do?" Emotion is of itself but a poor result unless it leads to practical action. To make men feel is well enough, but it must be a feeling which impels them to immediate movement, or at least to earnest enquiry as to what they shall do. O spirit of God, if Thou wilt rest on me, even, me, men shall not hear and go their way and forget what they have heard! They will arise and seek the Father, and taste His love. If Thou wouldst rest on all the brotherhood that publish Thy word men would not merely weep while they hear, and be affected while the discourage lasts, but they would go their way to ask, "What must we do to be saved?" This is what we need. We do not require new preachers, but we need a new anointing of the Spirit. We do not require novel forms of service, but we want the fire Spirit, the wind Spirit to work by us till everywhere men cry, "What must we do to be saved?"

Then came *a grand reception of the word*. We are told that they gladly received the word, and they received it in two senses: first, Peter bade them repent, and so they did. They were pricked to the heart from compunction on account of what they had done to Jesus, and they sorrowed after a godly sort, and quitted their sins. They also believed in Him whom they had slain, and accepted Him as their Saviour there and then, without longer hesitancy. They trusted in Him whom God had set forth to be a propitiation, and thus they fully received the word. Repentance and faith make up a complete reception of Christ, and they had both of these. Why should we not see this divine result to-day? We shall see it in proportion to our faith.

But what next? Why, they were *baptized* directly. Having repented and believed, the next step was to make confession of their faith; and they did not postpone that act for a single day ; why should they? Willing hands were there, the whole company of the faithful were all glad to engage in the holy service, and that same day were they baptized into the name of the Father, and of the Son, and of the Holy Spirit. If the Holy Ghost were fully with us, we should never have to complain that many believers never confess their faith, for they would be eager to confess the Saviour's name in His own appointed way. Backwardness to be baptized comes too often of fear of persecution, indecision, love of ease, pride, or disobedience; but all these vanish when the heavenly wind and fire are doing their sacred work. Sinful diffidence soon disappears, sinful shame of Jesus is no more seen, and hesitancy and delay are banished for ever when the Holy Spirit works with power.

Furthermore, there was not merely this immediate confession, but as a result of the Spirit of God there was *great steadfastness*. "They continued steadfastly in the apostles' doctrine." We have had plenty of revivals of the human sort, and their results have been sadly disappointing. Under excitement nominal converts have been multiplied: but where are they after a little testing? I am sadly compelled to own that, so far as I can observe, there has been much sown, and very little reaped that was worth reaping, from much of that which has been called revival. Our hopes were flattering as a dream; but the apparent result has vanished like a vision of the night. But where the Spirit of God is really at work the converts stand: they are well rooted and grounded, and hence they are not carried about by every wind of doctrine, but they continue steadfast in the apostolic truth.

We see next that there was *abundant worship of God*, for they were steadfast not only in the doctrine, but in breaking of bread, and in prayer, and in fellowship. There was no difficulty in getting a prayer meeting then, no difficulty in maintaining daily communion then, no want of holy fellowship then; for the Spirit of God was among them, and the ordinances were precious in their eyes. "Oh," say some, "if we could get this minister or that evangelist we should do well." Brothers, if you had the Holy Spirit you would have everything else growing out of His presence, for all good things are summed up in Him.

Next to this there came *striking generosity*. Funds were not hard to raise: liberality overflowed its banks, for believers poured all that they had into the common fund. Then was it indeed seen to be true that the silver and the gold are the Lord's. When the Spirit of God operates powerfully there is little need to issue telling appeals for widows and orphans, or go down on your knees and plead for missionary fields which cannot be occupied for want of money. When the Spirit of God comes, those who have substance yield it to their Lord: those who have but little grow rich by giving of that little, and those who are already rich become happy by consecrating what they have. There is no need to rattle the box when the rushing mighty wind is heard, and the fire is dissolving all hearts in love.

Then came *continual gladness*. "They did eat their meat with gladness." They were not merely glad at prayer-meetings and sermons, but glad at breakfast and at supper. Whatever they had to eat they were for singing over it. Jerusalem was the happiest city that ever was when the Spirit of God was there. The disciples were singing from morning to night, and I have no doubt the outsiders asked, "What is it all about?" The temple was never so frequented as then; there was never such singing before; the very streets of Jerusalem, and the Hill of Zion, rang with the songs of the once despised Galileans.

They were full of gladness, and that gladness showed itself in *praising God*. I have no doubt they broke out now and then in the services with shouts of, "Glory! Hallelujah!" I should not wonder but what all propriety was scattered to the winds. They were so glad, so exhilarated that they were ready to leap for joy. Of course we never say "Amen," or "Glory!" now. We have grown to be so frozenly proper that we never interrupt a service in any way, because, to tell the truth, we are not so particularly glad, we are not so specially full of praise that we want to do anything of the sort. Alas, we have lost very much of the Spirit of God, and much of the joy and gladness which attend His presence, and so we have settled into a decorous apathy! We gather the pinks of propriety instead of the palm branches of praise. God send us a season of glorious disorder. Oh for a sweep of wind that will set the seas in motion, and make our ironclad brethren now lying so quietly at anchor to roll from stem to stern. As for us, who are as the little ships, we will fly before the gale if it will but speed us to our desired haven. Oh for fire to fall again,—fire which shall affect the most stolid! This is a sure remedy for indifference. When a flake of fire falls into a man's bosom he knows it, and when the word of God comes home to a man's soul he knows it too. Oh that such fire might first sit upon the disciples and then fall on all around!

For, to close, there was then *a daily increase* of the church— "The Lord added to the church daily such as should be saved." Conversion was going on perpetually; additions to the church were not events which happened once a year, but they were everyday matters, "so mightily grew the word of God and prevailed." O Spirit of God, Thou art ready to work with us to-day even as Thou didst then! Stay not, we beseech Thee, but work at once. Break down every barrier that hinders the incoming of Thy might. Overturn, overturn, O sacred wind! Consume all obstacles, O heavenly fire, and give us now both hearts of flame and tongues of fire to preach thy reconciling word, for Jesus' sake. Amen.

THE INDWELLING AND OUTFLOWING OF THE HOLY SPIRIT

A Sermon

Text.—"He that believeth on me, as the scripture hath said, out of his belly shall flow rivers of living water. (But this spake he of the Spirit, which they that believe on him should receive: for the Holy Ghost was not yet given; because that Jesus was not yet glorified.)"—John vii. 38, 39.

"Nevertheless I tell you the truth; It is expedient for you that I go away: for if I go not away, the Comforter will not come unto you; but if I depart, I will send him unto you."—John xvi. 7.

It is essential, dear friends, that we should worship the living and true God. It will be ill for us if it can be said, "Ye worship ye know not what." "Thou shalt worship the Lord thy God, and him only shalt thou serve." The heathen err from this command by multiplying gods, and making this and that image to be the object of their adoration. Their excess runs to gross superstition and idolatry. I fear that sometimes we who "profess and call ourselves Christians" err in exactly the opposite direction. Instead of worshipping more than God I fear we worship less than God. This appears when we forget to pay due adoration to the Holy Spirit of God. The true God is triune, Father, Son, and Holy Spirit; and though there be but one God yet that one God has manifested Himself to us in the trinity of His sacred persons. If, then, I worship the Father and the Son, but forget or neglect to adore the Holy Spirit, I worship less than God. While the poor heathen in his ignorance goes far beyond and transgresses, I must take care lest I fall short and fail too.

What a grievous thing it will be if we do not pay that loving homage and reverence to the Holy Spirit which is so justly His due. May it not be the fact that we enjoy less of His power and see less of His working in the world because the church of God has not been sufficiently mindful of Him? It is a blessed thing to preach the work of Jesus Christ, but it is an evil thing to omit the work of the Holy Ghost; for the work of the Lord Jesus itself is no blessing to that man who does not know the work of the Holy Spirit. There is the ransom price, but it is only through the Spirit that we know the redemption: there is the precious blood, but it is as though the fountain had never been filled unless the Spirit of God lead us with repenting faith to wash therein. The bandage is soft and the ointment is effectual, but the wound will never be healed till the Holy Spirit shall apply that which the great Physician has provided. Let us not therefore be found neglectful of the work of the divine Spirit, lest we incur guilt, and inflict upon ourselves serious damage.

You that are believers have the most forcible reasons to hold the Holy Ghost in the highest esteem; for what are you now without Him? What were you, and what would you still have been, if it had not been for His gracious work upon you? He quickened you, else you had not been in the living family of God to-day. He gave you understanding that you might know the truth, else would you have been as ignorant as the carnal world is at this hour. It was He that awakened your conscience, convincing you of sin: it was He that gave you abhorrence of sin, and led you to repent: it was He that taught you to believe, and made you see that glorious Person who is to be believed, even Jesus, the Son of God. The Spirit has wrought in you your faith and love and hope, and every grace. There is not a jewel upon the neck of your soul which he did not place there.

> " For every virtue we possess,
>   And every victory won,
>   And every thought of holiness,
>   Are his alone."

Beloved brethren, notwithstanding all that the Spirit of God has already done in us, it is very possible that we have missed a large part of the blessing which He is willing to give, for He is able to "do exceeding abundantly above all that we ask or think." We have already come to Jesus, and we have drunk of the life-giving stream: our thirst is quenched, and we are made to live in Him. Is this all? Now that we are living in Him, and rejoicing to do so, have we come to the end of the matter? Assuredly not. We have reached as far as that first exhortation of the Master, "If any man thirst, let him come unto me and drink"; but do you think that the generality of the church of God have ever advanced to the next, "He that believeth on me, as the Scripture hath said, out of his belly shall flow rivers of living water"? I think I am not going beyond the grievous truth if I say that only here and there will you find men and women who have believed up to that point. Their thirst is quenched, as I have said, and they live, and because Jesus lives they shall live also, but health and vigour they have not: they have life, but they have not life more abundantly. They have little life with which to act upon others: they have no energy welling up and overflowing to go streaming out of them like rivers. Brothers, let us go in to get of God all that God will give us: let us set our heart upon this, that we mean to have by God's help all that the infinite goodness of God is ready to bestow. Let us not be satisfied with the sip that saves, but let us go on to the baptism which buries the flesh and raises us in the likeness of the risen Lord: even that baptism into the Holy Ghost and into fire which makes us spiritual and sets us all on flame with zeal for the glory of God and eagerness for usefulness by which that glory may be increased among the sons of men.

Thus I introduce you to my texts, and by their guidance we will enter upon the further consideration of the operations of the Holy Spirit, especially of those to which we would aspire.

I. We will commence with the remark that THE WORK OF THE SPIRIT IS INTIMATELY CONNECTED WITH THE WORK OF CHRIST. It is a great pity when persons preach the Holy Spirit's work so as to obscure the work of Christ; and I have known some do that, for they have held up before the sinner's eye the inward experience of believers, instead of lifting up first and foremost the crucified Saviour to whom we must look and live. The gospel is not "Behold the Spirit of God" but "Behold the Lamb of God." It is an equal pity when Christ is so preached that the Holy Spirit is ignored; as if faith in Jesus prevented the necessity of the new birth, and imputed righteousness rendered imparted righteousness needless. Have I not often reminded you that in the third chapter of John, where Jesus taught Nicodemus the doctrine, "Except a man be born again of water and of the spirit he cannot enter the kingdom of heaven," we also read those blessed words, "And as Moses lifted up the serpent in the wilderness, even so must the Son of man be lifted up: that whosoever believeth in Him should not perish, but have eternal life. For God so loved the world, that He gave His only begotten Son, that whosoever believeth in Him should not perish, but have everlasting life." The necessity for regeneration by the Spirit is there put very clearly, and so is the free promise that those who trust in Jesus shall be saved. This is what we ought to do: we must take care to let both these truths stand out most distinctly with equal prominence. They are intertwined with each other and are necessary each to each: what God hath joined together let no man put asunder.

They are so joined together that, first of all, *the Holy Spirit was not given until Jesus had been glorified*. Carefully note our first text; it is a very striking one: "This spake he of the Spirit which they that believe on Him should receive, for the Holy Ghost was not yet." The word "given" is not in the original: it is inserted by the translators to help out the sense, and they were perhaps wise in making such an addition, but the words are more forcible by themselves. How strong the statement, "For the Holy Ghost was not yet." Of course, we none of us dream that the Holy Spirit was not yet existing, for He is eternal and self-existent, being most truly God, but He was not yet in fellowship with man to the full extent in which He now is since Jesus Christ is glorified. The near and dear intercourse of God with man which is expressed by the indwelling of the Spirit could not take place till redeeming work was done and the Redeemer was exalted. As far as men were concerned, and the fulness of the blessing was concerned, indicated by the outflowing rivers of living water, the Spirit of God was not yet.

"Oh," say you, "but was not the Spirit of God in the church in the wilderness, and with the saints of God in all former ages?" I answer, Certainly, but not in the manner in which the Spirit of God now resides in the church of Jesus Christ. You read of the prophets, and of one and another gracious man, that the Spirit of God came upon them, seized them, moved them, spake by them; but He did not dwell in them. His operations upon men were a coming and a going: they were carried away by the Spirit of God, and came under His power, but the Spirit of God did not rest upon them or abide in them. Occasionally the sacred endowment of the Spirit of God came upon them, but they knew not "the communion of the Holy Ghost." As a French pastor very sweetly puts it, "He appeared unto men; He did not incarnate Himself in man. His actions was intermittent: He went and came, like the dove which Noah sent forth from the ark and which went to and fro, finding no rest; while in the new dispensation He dwells, He abides in the heart, as the dove, His emblem, which John the Baptist saw descending and alighting upon the head of Jesus. Affianced of the soul, the Spirit went off to see His betrothed, but was not yet one with her; the marriage was not consummated until the Pentecost after the glorification of Jesus Christ."

You know how our Lord puts it, "He dwelleth with you and shall be in you." That indwelling is another thing from being *with* us. The Holy Spirit was with the Apostles in the days when Jesus was with them; but He was not in them in the sense in which He filled them at and after the Day of Pentecost. This shows how intimately the gift of the Holy Ghost is connected with our Lord Jesus Christ, inasmuch as in the fullest sense of His indwelling the Holy Ghost would not be with us until Christ had been glorified. It has been well observed that our Lord sent out seventy evangelists to preach the gospel, even as He had aforetime sent out the twelve; and no doubt they preached with great zeal and produced much stir; but the Holy Ghost never took the trouble to preserve one of their sermons, or even the notes of one. I have not the slightest doubt that they were very crude and incomplete, showing more of human zeal than of divine unction, and hence they are forgotten; but no sooner had the Holy Spirit fallen than

Peter's first sermon is recorded, and henceforth we have frequent notes of the utterances of apostles, deacons and evangelists. There was an abiding fulness, and an overflowing of blessing, out of the souls of the saints after the Lord was glorified, which was not existing among men before that time.

Observe, too, that the Holy Spirit was given after the ascent of our divine Lord into His glory, partly *to make that ascent the more renowned*. When He ascended up on high He led captivity captive and gave gifts to men. These gifts were men in whom the Holy Spirit dwelt, who preached the gospel unto the nations. The shedding of the Holy Spirit upon the assembled disciples on that memorable day was the glorification of the risen Christ upon the earth. I know not in what way the Father could have made the glory of heaven so effectually to flow from the heights of the New Jerusalem and to come streaming down among the sons of men as by giving that chief of all gifts, the gift of the Holy Spirit when the Lord had risen and gone into His glory. With emphasis may I say of the Spirit at Pentecost that He glorified Christ by descending at such a time. What grander celebration could there have been? Heaven rang with hosannahs, and earth echoed the joy. The descending Spirit is the noblest testimony among men to the glory of the ascended Redeemer.

Was not the Spirit of God also sent at the time *as an evidence of our divine Master's acceptance*? Did not the Father thus say to the church, "My Son has finished the work, and has fully entered into his glory; therefore give I you of the Holy Spirit"? If you would know what a harvest is to come of the sowing of the bloody sweat and of the death wounds, see the first fruits. Behold how the Holy Spirit is given, Himself to be the first fruits, the earnest of the glory which shall yet be revealed in us. I want no better attestation from God of the finished work of Jesus than His blazing flaming seal of tongues of fire upon the heads of the disciples. He must have done His work, or such a boon as this would not have come from it.

Moreover, if you desire to see how the work of the Spirit come to us in connection with the work of Christ, recollect that *it is the Spirit's work to bear witness of Jesus Christ*. He does not take of a thousand different matters and show them to us, but he shall take "of mine," saith Christ, "and he shall show them unto you." The Spirit of God is engaged in a service in which the Lord Jesus Christ is the beginning and the end. He comes to men that they may come to Jesus. Hence He comes to convince us of sin that He may reveal the great sacrifice of sin: He comes to convince us of righteousness that we may see the righteousness of Christ; and of judgement that we may be prepared to meet Him when He shall come to judge the quick and dead.

It is by the gospel of Jesus Christ that the Spirit of God works in the hearts of men. "Faith cometh by hearing, and hearing by the word of God": the Holy Spirit uses the hearing of the word of God for the conviction, conversion, consolation, and sanctification of men. His usual and ordinary method of operation is to fasten upon the mind the things of God, and to put life and force into the consideration of them. He revives in men's memories things that have long been forgotten, and He frequently makes these the means of affecting the heart and conscience. The men can hardly recollect hearing these truths, but still they were heard by them at some time or other. Saving truths are such matters as are contained in their substance in the word of God, and lie within the range of the teaching, or the person, or work, or offices of our Lord Jesus Christ. It is the Spirit's one business here below to reveal Christ to us and in us, and to that work He steadily adheres.

Moreover, *the Holy Spirit's work is to conform us to the likeness of Jesus Christ.* He is not working us to this or that human ideal, but He is working us into the likeness of Christ that He may be the first-born among many brethren. Jesus Christ is that standard and model to which the Spirit of God by His sanctifying processes is bringing us till Christ be formed in us the hope of glory.

Evermore it is for the glory of Jesus that the Spirit of God works. He works not for the glory of a church or of a community: He works not for the honour of a man or for the distinction of a sect: His one great object is to glorify Christ. "He shall glorify me" is our Saviour's declaration, and when He takes of the things of Christ and shows them unto us, we are led more and more to reverence and love and adore our blessed Lord Jesus Christ.

II. We will now advance another step, and here we shall need our second text. THE OPERATIONS OF THE HOLY SPIRIT ARE OF INCOMPARABLE VALUE. They are of such incomparable value that the very best thing we can think of was not thought to be so precious as these are. Our Lord himself says, "It is expedient for you that I go away: for if I go not away, the Comforter will not come unto you." Beloved friends, the presence of Jesus Christ was of inestimable value to his disciples, and yet it was not such an advantage to his servants as the indwelling of the Holy Spirit. Is not this a wonderful statement? Well might our Lord preface it by saying, "Now I tell you the truth," as if He felt that they would find it a hard saying, for a hard saying it is. Consider for a moment what Christ was to His disciples while He was here, and then see what must be the value of the Spirit's operations when it is expedient that they should lose all that blessing in order to receive the Spirit of God.

Our Lord Jesus Christ was to them their teacher, they had learned everything from His lips: He was their leader, they had never to ask what to do, they had only to follow in His steps: He was their defender, whenever the Pharisees or Sadducees assailed them He was like a brazen wall to them: He was their comforter, in all times of grief they resorted to Him, and His dear sympathetic heart poured out floods of comfort at once. What if I were to say that the Lord Jesus Christ was everything to them, their all in all. What a father is to his children, ay, what a mother is to her suckling, that was Jesus Christ to His disciples; and yet the Spirit of God's abiding in the church is better even than all this.

Now take another thought. What would you think if Jesus Christ were to come among us now as in the days of His flesh: I mean not as He will come, but as He appeared at His first advent. What joy it would give you! Oh, the delights, the heavenly joys, to hear that Jesus Christ of Nazareth was on earth again, a man among men! Should we not clap our hands for joy? Our one question would be, "Master, where dwellest thou?" for we should all long to live just where he lived. We could then sympathize with the negroes when they flocked into Washington in large numbers to take up their residence there. Why, think you, did they come to live in that city? Because Massa Abraham Lincoln lived there who had set them free, and they thought it would be glorious to live as near as possible to their great friend. If Jesus lived anywhere, it would not matter where, if it were in the desert or on the bleakest of mountains, there would be a rush to the place. How would the spot be crowded; what rents they would pay for the worst of tenements if Jesus was but in the neighbourhood. But do you not see the difficulty? We could not all get near Him in any literal or corporeal fashion. Now that the church is multiplied into millions of believers, some of the Lord's followers would never be able to see him, and the most could only hope to speak with him now and then. In the days of His flesh the twelve might see Him every day, and so might the little company of disciples, but the case is altered now that multitudes are trusting in His name.

"But," you say, "surely it would thrill the church with enthusiasm." Fancy the Lord Himself standing on this platform this morning in the same garb as when He was upon earth. Oh, what rapturous worship! What burning zeal! What enthusiasm! We should go home in such a state of excitement as we never were in before. Yes, it is even so, but then the Lord is not going to carry on His kingdom by the force of mere mental excitement, not even by such enthusiasm as would follow the sight of His person. The work of the Holy Spirit is a truer work, a deeper work, a surer work, and will more effectually achieve the purposes of God than even would the enthusiasm to which we should be stirred by the bodily presence of our well-beloved Saviour. The work is to be spiritual, and therefore the visible presence has departed. It is better that it should be so. We must walk by faith, and by faith alone; how could we do this if we could see the Lord with these mortal eyes? This is the dispensation of the unseen Spirit, in which we render glory to God by trusting in His word, and relying upon the unseen energy. Now, faith works and faith triumphs though the world seeth not the foundation upon which faith is built, for the Spirit who works in us cannot be discerned by carnal minds: the world seeth Him not, neither knoweth Him.

Thus you see that the operations of the Holy Spirit must be inestimably precious. There is no calculating their value, since it is expedient that we lose the bodily presence of Christ rather than remain without the indwelling of the Spirit of God.

III. Now go back to my first text again and follow me in the third head. Those operations of the Spirit of God, of which I am afraid some Christians are almost ignorant, are of wondrous power. The text says, "He that believeth on Me, out of the midst of him shall flow rivers of living water." THESE OPERATIONS ARE OF MARVELLOUS POWER. Brethren, do you understand my text? Do rivers of living water flow out of you?

Notice, first, that this is to be *an inward work*: the rivers of living water are to flow out of the midst of the man. The words are according to our version, "Out of his belly"—that is, from his heart and soul. The rivers do not flow out of his mouth: the promised power is not oratory. We have had plenty of words, floods of words; but this is heart work. The source of the rivers is found in the inner life. It is an inward work at its fountain head. It is not a work of talent and ability, and show, and glitter, and glare: it is altogether an inward work. The life-flood is to come out of the man's inmost self, out of the bowels and essential being of the man. Homage is shown too generally to outward form and external observance, though these soon lose their interest and power; but when the Spirit of God rests within a man it exercises a home rule within him and he gives great attention to what an old divine was wont to call "the home department." Alas, many neglect the realm within which is the chief province under our care. O my brother in Christ, if you would be useful, begin with yourself. It is out of your very soul that a blessing must come. It cannot come out of you if it is not in you: and it cannot be in you unless God the Holy Ghost places it there.

Next, it is *life-giving* work. Out of the heart of the man, out of the centre of his life, are to flow rivers of living water; that is to say, he is instrumentally to communicate to others the divine life. When he speaks, when he prays, when he acts, he shall so speak and pray and act that there shall be going out of him an emanation which is full of the life of grace and godliness. He shall be a light by which others shall see. His life shall be the means of kindling life in other men's bosoms. "Out of his belly shall flow rivers of living water."

Note *the plenitude* of it. The figure would have been a surprising one, if it had said, "Out of him shall flow a river of living water"; but it is not so: it says rivers. Have you ever stood by the side of a very abundant spring? we have some such not far from London. You see the water bubbling up from many little mouths. Observe the sand dancing as the water forces its way from the bottom; and there, just across the road, a mill is turned by the stream which has just been created by he spring, and when the water-wheel is turned you see a veritable river flowing forward to supply Father Thames. Yet this is only one river; what would you think if you saw a spring yielding such supplies that a river flowed from it to the north, and a river to the south, a river to the east, and a river to the west; this is the figure before us: rivers of living water flowing out of the living man in all directions. What a word is this! Rivers of living water!! Oh that all professing Christians were such fountains.

See how *spontaneous* it is: "Out of the midst of him shall flow." No pumping is required; nothing is said about machinery and hydraulics; the man does not want exciting and stirring up, but, just as he is, influence of the best kind quietly flows away from him. Did you ever hear a great hubbub in the morning, a great outcry, a sounding of trumpets and drums, and did you ever ask, "What is it?" Did a voice reply, "The sun is about to rise, and he is making this noise that all may be aware of it"? No, he shines, but he has nothing to say about it; even so the genuine Christian just goes about flooding the world with blessing, and so far from claiming attention for himself, it may be that he himself is unconscious of what he is effecting. God so blesses him that his leaf does not wither, and whatsoever he doeth is prospering, for he is like a tree planted by the rivers of water that bringeth forth its fruit in its season: his verdure and fruit are the natural outcome of his vigorous life. Oh, the blessed spontaneity of the work of grace when a man gets into the fulness of it, for then he seems to eat and drink and sleep eternal life, and he spreads a savour of salvation all round.

And this is to be *perpetual*,—not like intermittent springs which burst forth and flow in torrents, and then cease,—but it is to be an everyday outgushing. In summer and winter, by day and by night, wherever the man is, he shall be a blessing. As he breathes, he shall breathe benedictions; as he thinks, his mind shall be devising generous things; and when he acts, his acts shall be as though the hand of God were working by the hand of man.

I hope I hear many sighs rising up in the place! I hope I hear friends saying, "Oh that I could get to that." I want you to attain the fulness of the favour. I pray that we may all get it; for because Jesus Christ is glorified therefore the Holy Spirit is given in this fashion, given more largely to those in the kingdom of heaven than to all those holy men before the Lord's ascent to His glory. God gives no stinted blessing to celebrate the triumph of His Son: God giveth not the Spirit by measure unto Him. On such an occasion heaven's grandest liberality was displayed. Christ is glorified in heaven above, and God would have Him glorified in the church below by vouchsafing a baptism of the Holy Ghost to each of us.

So I close by this, which I hope will be a very comforting and inspiriting reflection:—

IV. THESE OPERATIONS OF THE SPIRIT OF GOD ARE EASILY TO BE OBTAINED BY THE LORD'S CHILDREN. Did you say you had not received them? They are to be had, they are to be had at once. First, they are to be had by *believing in Jesus*. "This spake He of the Spirit, which they that believe on Him should receive." Do you not see that it is faith which gives us the first drink and causes us to live, and this second more abundant blessing of being ourselves made fountains from which rivers flow comes in the same way? Believe in Christ, for the blessing is to be obtained, not by the works of the law, nor by so much of fasting, and striving, and effort, but by belief in the Lord Jesus for it. With Him is the residue of the Spirit. He is prepared to give this to you, ay, to every one of you who believe on His name. He will not of course make all of you preachers; for who then would be hearers? If all were preachers the other works of the church would be neglected; but He will give you this favour, that out of you there shall stream a divine influence all round you to bless your children, to bless your servants, to bless the workmen in the house where you are employed, and to bless the street you live in. In proportion as God gives you opportunity these rivers of living water will flow in this channel and in that, and they will be pouring forth from you at all times, if you believe in Jesus for the full blessing, and can by faith receive it.

But there is another thing to be done as well, and that is *to pray*; and here I want to remind you of those blessed words of the Master, "Everyone that asketh receiveth; and he that seeketh findeth; and to him that knocketh it shall be opened. If a son shall ask bread of any of you that is a father, will he give him a stone? Or if he ask a fish, will he for a fish give him a serpent? Or if he shall ask an egg, will he offer him a scorpion? If ye then, being evil, know how to give good gifts unto your children: how much more shall your heavenly Father give the Holy Spirit to them that ask him?" You see, there is a distinct promise to the children of God, that their heavenly Father will give them the Holy Spirit if they ask for His power; and that promise is made to be exceedingly strong by the instances joined to it. But he says, "*How much more* shall your heavenly Father give the Holy Spirit to them that ask him?" He makes it a stronger case than that of an ordinary parent. The Lord must give us the Spirit when we ask Him, for He has herein bound Himself by no ordinary pledge. He has used a simile which would bring dishonour on His own name, and that of the very grossest kind, if He did not give the Holy Spirit to them that ask Him.

Oh, then, let us ask Him at once, with all our hearts. Am I not so happy as to have in this audience some who will immediately ask? I pray that some who have never received the Holy Spirit at all may now be led, while I am speaking, to pray, "Blessed Spirit, visit me; lead me to Jesus." But especially those of you that are the children of God,—to you is this promise especially made. Ask God to make you all that the Spirit of God can make you, not only a satisfied believer who has drunk for himself, but a useful believer, who overflows the neighbourhood with blessing. I see here a number of friends from the country who have come to spend their holiday in London. What a blessing it would be if they went back to their respective churches overflowing; for there are numbers of churches that need flooding; they are dry as a barn-floor, and little dew ever falls on them. Oh that they might be flooded!

What a wonderful thing a flood is! Go down to the river, look over the bridge, and see the barges and other craft lying in the mud. All the king's horses and all the king's men cannot tug them out to sea. There they lie, dead and motionless as the mud itself. What shall we do with them? What machinery can move them? Have we a great engineer among us who will devise a scheme for lifting these vessels and bearing them down to the river's mouth? No, it cannot be done. Wait till the tide comes in! What a change! Each vessel walks the water like a thing of life. What a difference between the low tide and the high tide. You cannot stir the boats when the water is gone; but when the tide is at the full see how readily they move; a little child may push them with his hand. Oh, for a flood of grace! The

Lord send to all our churches a great springtide! Then the indolent will be active enough, and those who were half dead will be full of energy. I know that in this particular dock several vessels are lying that I should like to float, but I cannot stir them. They neither work for God nor come out to the prayer-meetings, nor give of their substance to spread the gospel. If the flood would come you would see what they are capable of: they would be active, fervent, generous, abounding in every good word and work. So may it be! So may it be! May springs begin to flow in all our churches, and may all of you who hear me this day get your share of the streams. Oh that the Lord may now fill you and then send you home bearing a flood of grace with you. It sounds oddly to speak of a man's carrying home a flood within him, and yet I hope it will be so, and that out of you shall flow rivers of living water. So may God grant for Jesus' sake. Amen.

THE ABIDING OF THE SPIRIT THE GLORY OF THE CHURCH

A SERMON

Text.—"Yet now be strong, O Zerubbabel, saith the Lord; and be strong, O Joshua, son of Josedech, the high priest; and be strong, all ye people of the land, saith the Lord, and work: for I am with you, saith the Lord of hosts: according to the word that I covenanted with you when ye came out of Egypt, so my spirit remaineth among you: fear ye not."—Haggai ii, 4, 5.

SATAN is always doing his utmost to stay the work of God. He hindered these Jews from building the temple; and to-day he endeavours to hinder the people of God from spreading the gospel. A spiritual temple is to be builded for the Most High, and if by any means the evil one can delay its uprising he will stick at nothing: if he can take us off from working with faith and courage for the glory of God he will be sure to do it. He is very cunning, and knows how to change his argument and yet keep to his design: little cares he how he works, so long as he can hurt the cause of God.

In the case of the Jewish people on their return from captivity he sought to prevent the building of the temple by making them selfish and worldly, so that every man was eager to build his own house, and cared nothing for the house of the Lord. Each family pleaded its own urgent needs. In returning to a long-deserted and neglected land, much had to be done to make up for lost time; and to provide suitably for itself every family needed all its exertions. They carried this thrift and self-providing to a great extreme, and secured for themselves luxuries, while the foundations of the temple which had been laid years before remained as they were, or became still more thickly covered up with rubbish. The people could not be made to bestir themselves to build a house of God, for they answered to every exhortation, "The time is not come, the time that the Lord's house should be built." A more convenient season was always looming in the future, but it never came. Just now it was too hot, further on it was too cold; at one time the wet season was just setting in and it was of no use to begin, and soon after the fair weather required that they should be in their own fields. Like some in our day, they saw to themselves first, and God's turn was very long in coming; hence the prophet cried, "Is it time for you, O ye, to dwell in your ceiled houses, and this house lie waste?"

By the mouth of his servant Haggai stern rebukes were uttered, and the whole people were aroused. We read in verse twelve of the first chapter, "Then Zerubbabel the son of Shealtiel, and Joshua the son of Josedech, the high priest, with all the remnant of the people, obeyed the voice of the Lord their God, and the words of Haggai the prophet, as the Lord their God had sent him, and the people did fear before the Lord." All hands were put to the work; course after course of stone began to rise; and then another stumbling-block was thrown in the way of the workers. The older folks remarked that this was a very small affair compared with the temple of Solomon, of which their fathers had told them; in fact, their rising building was nothing at all, and not worthy to be called a temple.

The prophet describes the feeling in the verse which precedes our text. "Who is left among you that saw this house in her first glory? and how do ye see it now? is it not in your eyes in comparison of it as nothing?" Feeling that their work would be very poor and insignificant, the people had little heart to go on. Being discouraged by the humiliating contrast, they began to be slack; and as they were quite willing to accept any excuse, and here was an excuse ready made for them, they would soon have been at a standstill had not the prophet met the wiles of the arch-enemy with another word from the Lord. Nothing so confounds the evil one as the voice of the Eternal. Our Lord himself defeated Satan by the word of the Lord; and the prophet Haggai did the same. Twice the voice was heard—"*I am with you, saith the Lord of hosts.*" They were also assured that what they builded was accepted, and that the Lord meant to fill the new house with glory; yea, He meant to light it up with a glory greater than that which honoured the temple of Solomon. They were not spending their strength for nought, but were labouring with divine help and favour. Thus they were encouraged to put their shoulders to the work: the walls rose in due order, and God was glorified in the building up of His Zion.

The present times are, in many respects, similar to those of Haggai. History certainly repeats itself within the church of God as well as outside of it; and therefore the messages of God need to be repeated also. The words of some almost-forgotten prophet may be re-delivered by the watchman of the Lord in these present days, and be a timely word for the present emergency. We are not free from the worldliness which put self first and God nowhere, else our various enterprises would be more abundantly supplied with the silver and the gold which are the Lord's, but which even professing Christians reserve for themselves. When this selfish greed is conquered, then comes in a timorous depression. Among those who have escaped from worldliness there is apt to be too much despondency, and men labour feebly as for a cause which is doomed to failure. This last evil must be cured. I pray that our text may this morning flame from the Lord's own mouth with all the fire which once blazed about it. May faint heart be encouraged and drowsy spirits be aroused, as we hear the Lord say, "*My spirit remaineth among you: fear ye not.*"

I shall enter fully upon the subject, by the assistance of the Holy Spirit, by calling your attention to *discouragement forbidden.* Then I shall speak of *encouragement imparted*; and, having done so, I shall linger with this blessed text which overflows with comfort, and shall speak, in the third place, of *encouragement further applied.* Oh that our Lord, who knows how to speak a word in season to him that is weary, may cheer the hearts of seekers by what shall be spoken under this last head of discourse!

I. To begin with, here is DISCOURAGEMENT FORBIDDEN. Discouragement comes readily enough to us poor mortals who are occupied in the work of God, seeing it is a work of faith, a work of difficulty, a work above our capacity, and a work much opposed.

Discouragement is very natural: it is a native of the soil of manhood. To believe is supernatural, faith is the work of the Spirit of God; to doubt is natural to fallen men; for we have within us an evil heart of unbelief. It is abominably wicked, I grant you; but still it is natural, because of the downward tendency of our depraved hearts.

Discouragement may come and does come to us, as it did to these people, from a consideration of the great things which God deserves at our hands, and the small things which we are able to render. When in Haggai's days the people thought of Jehovah, and of a temple for Him, and then looked upon the narrow space which had been enclosed, and the common stones which had been laid for foundations, they were ashamed. Where were those hewn stones and costly stones which, of old, Solomon brought from far? They said within themselves, "This house is unworthy of Jehovah: what do we by labouring thus?" Have you not felt the depressing weight of what is so surely true? Brethren, all that we do is little for our God; far too little for Him that loved us and gave Himself for us. For Him that poured out His soul unto death on our behalf the most splendid service, the most heroic self-denial, are all too little; and we feel it is so. Alabaster boxes of precious ointment are too mean a gift. When we have done our utmost in declaring the glory of Jesus, we have felt that words are too poor and mean to set forth our adorable Lord.

When we have prayed for His kingdom we have been disgusted with our own prayers; and all the efforts we have put forth in connection with any part of His service have seemed too few, too feeble for us to hope for acceptance. Thus have we been discouraged. The enemy has worked upon us by this means, yet he has made us argue very wrongly. Because we could not do much, we have half resolved to do nothing! Because what we did was so poor, we were inclined to quit the work altogether! This is evidently absurd and wicked. The enemy can use humility for his purpose as well as pride. Whether he makes us think too much or too little of our work, it is all the same so long as he can get us off from it.

It is significant that the man with one talent went and hid his Lord's money in the earth. He knew that it was but one, and for that reason he was the less afraid to bury it. Perhaps he argued that the interest on one talent could never come to much, and would never be noticed side by side with the result of five or ten talents; and he might as well bring nothing at all to his Lord as bring so little. Perhaps he might not have wrapped it up if it had not been so small that a napkin could cover it. The smallness of our gifts may be a temptation to us. We are consciously so weak and so insignificant, compared with the great God and His great cause, that we are discouraged, and think it vain to attempt anything.

Moreover, the enemy contrasts our work with that of others and with that of those who have gone before us. We are doing so little as compared with other people, therefore let us give up. We cannot build like Solomon, therefore let us not build at all. Yet, brethren, there is a falsehood in all this; for, in truth, nothing is worthy of God. The great works of others, and even the amazing productions of Solomon, all fell short of His glory. What house could man build for God? What are cedar, and marble, and gold as compared with the glory of the Most High? Though the house was "exceeding magnifical," yet the Lord God has of old dwelt within curtains, and never was His worship more glorious than within the tent of badgers' skins; indeed, as soon as the great house was built, true religion declined. What of all human work can be worthy of the Lord? Our little labours do but share the insignificance of greater things, and therefore we ought not to withhold them: yet here is the temptation from which we must pray to be delivered.

The tendency to depreciate the present because of the glories of the past is also injurious. The old people looked back to the days of the former temple, even as we are apt to look upon the times of the great preachers of the past. What work was done in those past days! What Sabbaths were enjoyed then! What converts were added to the church! What days of refreshing were then vouchsafed! Everything has declined, decreased, degenerated!

But, brethren, we must not allow this sense of littleness to hamper us; for God can bless our littleness, and use it for His glory. I notice that the great men of the past thought of themselves even as we think of ourselves. Certainly they were not more self-confident than we are. Let us throw our heart and soul into the work of the Lord, and yet do something more nearly in accordance with our highest ideal of what our God deserves of us. Let us excel our ancestors. Let us aspire to be even more godly, more conscientious, and more sound in the faith than they were, for the Spirit of God remaineth with us.

Wherever discouragement comes in it is dreadfully weakening. I am sure it is weakening, because the prophet was bidden to say three times to the governor, high priest, and people, "Be strong." This proves that they had become weak. Being discouraged, their hands hung down, and their knees were feeble. Faith girds us with omnipotence, but unbelief makes everything hang loose and limp about us. Distrust, and thou wilt fail in everything; believe and according to thy faith so shall it be unto thee. To lead a discouraged people to the Holy War is as difficult as for Xerxes' commanders to conduct the Persian troops to battle against the Greeks. The vassals of the great king were driven to the conflicts by whips and sticks, for they were afraid to fight: do you wonder that they were defeated? A church that needs constant exhorting and compelling accomplishes nothing. The Greeks had no need of blows and threats, for each man was a lion, and courted the encounter, however great the odds against him. Each Spartan fought *con amore*; he was never more at home than when contending for the altars and the hearths of his country. We want Christian men of this same sort, who have faith in their principles, faith in the doctrines of grace, faith in God the Father, God the Son, and God the Holy Ghost; and who therefore contend earnestly for the faith in these days when piety is mocked at from the pulpit, and the gospel is sneered at by professional preachers. We need men who love the truth, to whom it is dear as their lives; men into whose hearts the old doctrine is burned by the hand of God's Spirit through a deep experience of its necessity and of its power. We need no more of those who will parrot what they are taught, but we want men who will speak what they know. Oh, for a troop of men like John Knox, heroes of the martyr and covenanter stock! Then would Jehovah of hosts have a people to serve Him who would be strong in the Lord and in the power of His might.

Discouragement not only weakens men, but *it takes them off from the service of God.* It is significant that the prophet said to them, "Be strong, all ye people of the land, saith the Lord, *and work.*" They had ceased to build: they had begun to talk and argue, but they had laid down the trowel. They were extremely wise in their observations, and criticisms, and prophecies; but the walls did not rise. It is always so when we are discouraged: we cease from the work of the Lord, and waste time in talk and nonsensical refinements. May the Lord take away discouragement from any of you who now suffer from it! I suppose some of you feel it, for at times it creeps over my heart and makes me go with heaviness to my work. I believe that God's truth will come to the front yet, but it hath many adversaries to-day. All sorts of unbeliefs are being hatched out from under the wings of "modern thought." The gospel seems to be regarded as a nose of wax, to be altered and shaped by every man who wishes to show his superior skill. Nor is it in doctrine alone, but in practise also, that the times are out of joint. Separateness from the world, and holy living, are to give place to gaiety and theatregoing. To follow Christ fully has gone out of fashion with many of those from whom we once hoped better things. Yet are there some who waver not, some who are willing to be in the right with two or three. Blessed is the man who shall be able to stand fast by his God in these evil days. Let us not in any wise be discouraged. "Be strong; be strong; be strong," sounds as a threefold voice from the triune God. "Fear not" comes as a sweet cordial to the faint: therefore let no man's heart fail him. Thus much about the discouragement.

II. Secondly, here is THE ENCOURAGEMENT IMPARTED, which is the grand part of our text. "According to the word that I covenanted with you when ye came out of Egypt, so my spirit remaineth among you: fear ye not." God remembers His covenant and stands to His ancient promises. When the people came out of Egypt the Lord was with them by His Spirit: hence He spoke to them by Moses, and through Moses He guided, and judged, and taught them. He was with them also by His Spirit in inspiring Bezaleel and Aholiab, as to the works of art which adorned the tabernacle. God always finds workmen for his work, and by His Spirit fits them for it. The Spirit of God rested upon the elders who were ordained to relieve Moses of his great burden.

The Lord was also with His people in the fiery cloudy pillar which was conspicuous in the midst of the camp. His presence was their glory and their defence. This is a type of the presence of the Spirit with the church. At the present day, if we hold the truth of God, if we live in obedience to His holy commands, if we are spiritually-minded, if we cry unto God in believing prayer, if we have faith in His covenant and in His Son, the Holy Spirit abideth among us. The Holy Ghost descended upon the church at Pentecost, and He has never gone back again: there is no record of the Spirit's return to heaven. He will abide with the true church evermore. This is our hope for the present struggle. The Spirit of God remaineth with us.

To what end, my brethren, is this Spirit with us? Let us think of this, that we may be encouraged at this time. The Spirit of God remaineth among you *to aid and assist the ministry which He has already given*. Oh, that the prayers of God's people would always go up for God's ministers, that they may speak with a divine power and influence which none shall be able to gainsay! We look too much for clever men; we seek out fluent and flowery speakers; we sigh for men cultured and trained in all the knowledge of the heathen: nay, but if we sought more for unction, for divine authority, and for that power which doth hedge about the man of God, how much wiser should we be! Oh, that all of us who profess to preach the gospel would learn to speak in entire dependence upon the direction of the Holy Spirit, not daring to utter our own words, but even trembling lest we should do so, and committing ourselves to that secret influence without which nothing will be powerful upon the conscience or converting to the heart.

Know ye not the difference between the power that cometh of human oratory, and that which cometh by the divine energy which speaks so to the heart that men cannot resist it? We have forgotten this too much. It were better to speak six words in the power of the Holy Ghost than to preach seventy years of sermons without the Spirit. He who rested on those who have gone to their reward in heaven can rest this day upon our ministers and bless our evangelists, if we will but seek it of Him. Let us cease to grieve the Spirit of God, and look to Him for help to the faithful ministers who are yet spared to us.

This same Spirit who of old gave to His church eminent teachers *can raise up other and more useful men*. The other day, a brother from Wales told me of the great men he remembered: he said that he had never heard such a one as Christmas Evans, who surpassed all men when he was in the *hwyl*. I asked him if he knew another Welsh minister who preached like Christmas Evans. "No," he said, "we have no such man in Wales in our days." So in England we have neither Wesley nor Whitefield, nor any of their order; yet, as with God is the residue of the Spirit, He can fetch out from some chimney-corner another Christmas Evans, or find in our Sunday-school another George

Whitefield, who shall declare the gospel with the Holy Ghost sent down from heaven. Let us never fear for the future, to despair for the present, since the Spirit of God remaineth with us. What if the growing error of the age should have silenced the last tongue that speaks out the old gospel, let not faith be weakened. I hear the tramp of legions of soldiers of the cross. I hear the clarion voices of hosts of preachers. "The Lord gave the word; great was the company of those that published it." Have faith in God through our Lord Jesus Christ! When He ascended on high He led captivity captive, and received gifts for men. He then gave apostles, teachers, preachers and evangelists, and He can do the like again. Let us fall back upon the eternal God, and never be discouraged for an instant.

Nor is this all. The Holy Spirit being with us, *He can move the whole church to exercise its varied ministries*. This is one of the things we want very much—that every member of the church should recognise that he is ordained to service. Everyone in Christ, man or woman, hath some testimony to bear, some warning to give, some deed to do in the name of the holy child Jesus; and if the Spirit of God be poured out upon our young men and our maidens, each one will be aroused to energetic service. Both small and great will be in earnest, and the result upon the slumbering masses of our population will surprise us all. Sometimes we lament that the churches are so dull. There is an old proverb which says of So-and-so, that he was "as sound asleep as a church." I suppose there is nothing that can sleep so soundly as a church. But yet the Spirit of God still remaineth, and therefore churches go to be awakened. I mean that not only in part but as a whole, a church may be quickened. The dullest professor, the most slovenly believer, the most captious and useless member of a church. may yet be turned to good account. I see them like a stack of faggots, piled up, dead, and dry. Oh for the fire! We will have a blaze out of them yet.

Come, Holy Spirit, heavenly Dove, brood over the dark, disordered church as once Thou didst over chaos, and order shall come out of confusion, and the darkness shall fly before the light. Only let the Spirit be with us, and we have all that is wanted for victory. Give us His presence, and everything else will come in its due season for the profitable service of the entire church.

If the Spirit be with us, there will come multitudinous conversions. We cannot get at "the lapsed masses," as they are pedantically called. We cannot stir the crass infidelity of the present age: no, *we* cannot, but *He* can. All things are possible with God. If you walk down to our bridges at a certain hour of the day you will see barges and vessels lying in the mud; and all the king's horses and all the king's men cannot stir them. Wait until the tide comes in, and they will walk the water like things of life. The living flood accomplishes at once what no mortals can do. And so to-day our churches cannot stir. What shall we do? Oh, that the Holy Spirit would come with a flood-tide of His benign influences, as He will if we will but believe in Him; as He must if we will but cry unto Him; as He shall if we will cease to grieve Him. Everything will be even as the saints desire when the Lord of saints is with us. The hope of the continuance and increase of the church lies in the remaining of the Spirit with us. The hope of the salvation of London lies in the wonder-working Spirit. Let us bow our heads and worship the omnipotent Spirit who deigns to work in us, by us, and with us.

Then, brethren, if this should happen—and I see not why it should not—then we may expect to see *the church put on her beautiful garments;* then shall she begin to clear herself of the errors which now defile her; then shall she press to her bosom the truths which she now begins to forget; then will she go back to the pure fount of inspiration and drink from the Scriptures of truth; and then out of the midst of her shall flow no turbid streams, but rivers of living water. If the Holy Ghost will work among us we shall rejoice in the Lord, and glory in the name of our God.

When once the Spirit of God putteth forth His might all things else will be in accord with Him. Notice that in the rest of the chapter—which I shall read now, not as relating to that temple at all, but to the church of God—there is great comfort given to us. If the Holy Spirit be once given, then we may expect providence to co-operate with the church of God. Read verse 6: "Yet once, it is a little while, and I will shake heaven and the earth, and the sea, and the dry land. I will shake all nations." Great commotions will co-operate with the Holy Spirit. We may expect that God will work for His people in an extraordinary fashion if they will but be faithful to Him. Empires will collapse, and times will change, for the truth's sake. Expect the unexpected, reckon upon that which is unlikely, if it be necessary for the growth of the kingdom. Of old the earth helped the woman when the dragon opened his mouth to drown her with the floods that he cast forth: unexpected help shall come to us when affairs are at their worst.

And next, the Lord in this chapter promises His people that they shall have all the supplies they need for His work. They feared that they could not build His house, because of their poverty; but, saith the Lord of hosts, "The silver and the gold are mine." When the church of God believes in God, and goes forward bravely, she need not trouble as to supplies. Her God will provide for her. He that gives the Holy Ghost will give gold and silver according as they are needed; therefore let us be of good courage. If God is with us, why need we fear? One of our English kings once threatened the great city of London that if its councillors talked so independently, he would—yes—he would, indeed he would—take his court away from the city. The Lord Mayor on that occasion replied, that if his majesty would graciously leave the river Thames behind him, the citizens would try to get on without his court. If any say, "If you hold to these old-fashioned doctrines you will lose the educated, the wealthy, the influential," we answer: But if we do not lose the godly and the presence of the Holy Ghost we are not in the least alarmed. If the Holy Ghost remaineth with us, there is a river the streams whereof make glad the city of God. Brethren, my heart leaps within me as I cry, "The Lord of hosts is with us; the God of Jacob is our refuge." "Therefore will we not fear, though the earth be removed, and though the mountains be carried into the midst of the sea."

The best comfort of all remained: "The desire of all nations shall come." This was in a measure fulfilled when Jesus came into that latter house and caused all holy hearts to sing for gladness; but it was not wholly fulfilled in that way; for if you notice in the ninth verse it is written, "The glory of this latter house shall be greater than of the former; *and in this place will I give peace*," which the Lord did not fully do to the second temple, since that was destroyed by the Romans. But there is another advent, when "the desire of all nations shall come" in power and glory; and this is our highest hope. Though truth may be driven back, and error may prevail, Jesus comes, and He is the great Lord and patron of truth: He shall judge the world in righteousness, and the people in equity. Here is our last resource; here are God's reserves. He whom we serve liveth and reigneth for ever and ever; and He saith, "Behold, I come quickly; and my reward is with me, to give every man according as his work shall be." "Therefore, my beloved brethren, be ye stedfast, unmoveable, always abounding in the work of the Lord, forasmuch as ye know that your labour is not in vain in the Lord."

III. I should have done if it had not been that this text seemed to me to overflow so much, that it might not only refresh God's people, but give drink to thirsty sinners who are seeking the Lord. For a moment or two I give myself to ENCOURAGEMENT FURTHER APPLIED.

I

It is at the beginning of every gracious purpose that men have most fear, even as these people had who had newly begun to build. When first the Holy Spirit begins to strive with a man and to lead him to Jesus, he is apt to say—"I cannot; I dare not; it is impossible. How can I believe and live?" Now I want to speak to some of you here who are willing to find Christ, and to encourage you by the truth that the Spirit lives to help you. I would even like to speak to those who are *not* anxious to be saved. I remember that Dr. Payson, an exceedingly earnest and useful man of God, once did a singular thing. He had been holding inquiry meetings with all sorts of people, and great numbers had been saved. At last, one Sunday he gave out that he should have a meeting on Monday night of those persons who did not desire to be saved; and, strange to say, some twenty persons came who did not wish to repent or believe. He spoke to them and said, "I am sure that if a little film, thin as the web of the gossamer, were let down by God from heaven to each one of you, you would not push it away from you. Although it were almost invisible, you would value even the slightest connection between you and heaven. Now, your coming to meet me to-night is a little link with God. I want it to increase in strength till you are joined to the Lord for ever." He spoke to them most tenderly, and God blessed those people who did not desire to be saved, so that before the meeting was over they were of another mind. The film had become a thicker thread, and it grew and grew until the Lord Christ held them by it for ever.

Dear friends, the fact of your being in the Tabernacle this morning is like that filmy thread: do not put it away. Here is your comfort, the Holy Spirit still works with the preaching of the word. Do I hear you say, "I cannot feel my need of Christ as I want to feel it?" The Spirit remaineth among us. He can make you feel more deeply the guilt of sin and your need of pardon. "But I have heard so much about conviction and repentance; I do not seem to have either of them." Yet the Spirit remaineth with us, and that Spirit is able to work in you the deepest conviction and the truest repentance. "O sir, I do not feel as if I could do anything": but the Spirit remaineth with us, and all things that are needful for godliness He can give. He can work in you to will and to do of His own good pleasure. "But I want to believe in the Lord Jesus Christ unto eternal life." Who made you want to do that? Who but the Holy Spirit? Therefore He is still at work with you; and though as yet you do not understand what believing is, or else I am persuaded you would believe at once, the Spirit of God can instruct you in it. You are blind, but He can give you sight; you are paralyzed, but He can give you strength—the Spirit of God remaineth.

"Oh, but that doctrine of regeneration staggers me: you know, we must be born again." Yes, we are born again of the Spirit, and the Spirit remaineth still with us; He is still mighty to work that wondrous change, and to bring you out of the kingdom of Satan into the kingdom of God's dear Son. The Spirit remaineth with us, blessed be His name! "Ah, dear sir," says one, "I want to conquer sin!" Who made you desire to conquer sin? Who, but the Spirit that remaineth with us? He will give you the sword of the Spirit and teach you how to use it, and He will give you both the will and the power to use it successfully. Through the Spirit's might you can overcome every sin, even that which has dragged you down and disgraced you. The Spirit of God is still waiting to help you. When I think of the power of the Spirit of God, I look hopefully upon every sinner here this morning. I bless His name that He can work in you all that is pleasing in His sight. Some of you may be very careless but He can make you thoughtful. Coming up to London to see the Exhibition, I hope you may yourselves become an exhibition of divine grace. You think not about things, but He can make you feel at this moment a sweet softness stealing over you, until you long to be alone and to get home to the old armchair and there seek the Lord. You can thus be led to salvation.

I thought when I came in here that I should have a picked congregation; and so I have. You are one of them. Wherever you come from, I want you now to seek the Lord. He has brought you here, and He means to bless you. Yield yourselves to Him while His sweet Spirit pleads with you. While the heavenly wind softly blows upon you open wide every window. You have not felt that you wanted it; but that is the sure proof that you need it; for he that does not know his need of Christ, is most in need. Open wide your heart that the Spirit may teach you your need; above all, breathe the prayer that He would help you this morning to look to the Lord Jesus Christ, for "there is life in a look at the Crucified One—there is life at this moment for you."

"Oh," you say, "if I were to begin I should not keep on." No; if *you* began perhaps you would not; but if *He* begins with you *He* will keep on. The final perseverance of saints is the result of the final perseverance of the Holy Spirit; He perseveres to bless, and we persevere in receiving the blessing. If He begins, you have begun with a divine power that fainteth not neither is weary. I wish it might so happen that on this fifth day of the ninth month, not the prophet Haggai, but I, God's servant, may have spoken to you such a word as you shall never forget; and may the Lord add to the word, by the witness of the Holy Ghost,

"From this day will I bless you!" Go away with that promise resting upon you. I would like to give a shake of the hand to every stranger here this morning, and say, "Brother, in the name of the Lord I wish you from this day a blessing." Amen and amen.